Introduction to Networking Using NetWare (4.1)

Nancy B. Velasco

Computer Learning Center, Anaheim, CA

Prentice Hall
Upper Saddle River, New Jersey   Columbus, Ohio

Library of Congress Cataloging-in-Publication Data

Velasco, Nancy B.
  Introduction to networking using NetWare (4.1) / Nancy B. Velasco.
    p. cm.
  Includes index.
  ISBN 0-13-235938-3
    1. Netware.   2. Operating systems (Computers)   3. Local area
networks (Computer networks)   I. Title.
QA76.76.063V42   1997
005.7'1369–dc20   96-17704
                                                                   CIP

Cover photo: William J. Warren/H. Armstrong Roberts
Editor: Charles E. Stewart, Jr.
Production Editor: Stephen C. Robb
Design Coordinator: Julia Zonneveld Van Hook
Cover Designer: Russ Maselli
Production Manager: Deidra M. Schwartz
Marketing Manager: Debbie Yarnell

This book was set in Times Roman and Univers by Bi-Comp, Inc. and was printed and
bound by Quebecor Printing/Book Press. The cover was printed by Phoenix Color Corp.

 © 1997 by Prentice-Hall, Inc.
Simon & Schuster/A Viacom Company
Upper Saddle River, New Jersey 07458

Printed in the United States of America

10 9 8 7 6 5 4 3 2 1

ISBN: 0-13-235938-3

Prentice-Hall International (UK) Limited, *London*
Prentice-Hall of Australia Pty. Limited, *Sydney*
Prentice-Hall Canada, Inc., *Toronto*
Prentice-Hall Hispanoamericana, S. A., *Mexico*
Prentice-Hall of India Private Limited, *New Delhi*
Prentice-Hall of Japan, Inc., *Tokyo*
Simon & Schuster Asia Pte. Ltd., *Singapore*
Editora Prentice-Hall do Brasil, Ltda., *Rio de Janeiro*

In loving memory of my parents
Ida Mae Blackmon
and
Tollie Zack Blackmon
who taught me to value the learning
opportunities that come my way
and to enjoy life
and the Creator of life

PREFACE

Introduction to Networking Using NetWare 4.1 is an essential guide for anyone new to networking or anyone needing a quick refresher or overview. It's also an excellent resource for people who do not have weeks to sift through technical manuals and traditional networking books. This book, written in a down-to-earth, concise style, seeks to speed up the learning process and improve retention of the concepts learned.

Networking is no longer something of the future. In our mobile society, networking ties together people from all walks of life. Within a company, networking enables workers to communicate without even leaving their desks; thus the term *paperless society* came into vogue. Networks allow users to share hardware and software, which cuts down on the expenditures of the company. Networking also allows users to share customer databases, thus cutting down on repetitiveness and increasing accuracy. Novell NetWare currently ranks as the network operating system that most companies choose to implement at the installation site. Personnel who can work with a local area network (LAN) to set up user accounts, troubleshoot, and manage day-to-day tasks become a valuable asset to a company. The goal of this book is to help the readers do just that—by providing the resources that they need to excel in their careers.

Some of the important features of this book are as follows:

- *Introduction to networking components, jargon, and common usage.* This discussion looks at the ingredients for making a small-size LAN and introduces terms commonly used in the networking industry.
- *Setting up and managing the user's workstation.* This book covers how the local operating system (such as DOS) and the network operating system (NOS) interrelate. It discusses the steps needed to set up a workstation on the network and to

log in to the network. It also covers a helpful review of the major DOS commands used at the local level.

- *Novell Directory Services (NDS)*. Working with files and directories is at the heart of NetWare; thus this book emphasizes this area. This book explores the structure of Novell Directory Services, gives helpful suggestions on setting up and managing the NDS, and explores many utilities required for such management.
- *Managing user accounts and providing for security*. Setting up users on the network, assigning rights, and taking other safeguard measures are important to the network's overall security and daily operation. This book explores various utilities available for managing the network.
- *Communicating and printing*. This book looks at ways of communicating on the network and also discusses printer setups and the printing of reports.
- *Automating the user's work environment*. This book explains how to create login scripts and menus. These two tools automate a user's work environment and lessens the amount of training and associated errors common for first-time users.

Network Courtesy

As with most industries, the networking profession has a code of conduct that is unspoken yet expected of all users on the system. Review the following courtesy rules before starting your networking adventure:

1. Administrators need to find out from users what their needs are. Administrators should politely explain that they want to ensure that the network working environment is sufficient for all users.
2. Administrators need to let the users know that they are available if problems are encountered, especially problems about accessing software and updating customer accounts.
3. Administrators need to follow up with users of new accounts to ensure that those users are not experiencing any problems with the system. If they are experiencing problems, the administrator should find the cause and the solution for each problem. Sometimes, it may be necessary to increase rights in a given directory, but this should be done cautiously.
4. All users should remember to respect other users' workspace bubble when sending messages. Users should keep messages on a professional level and avoid cluttering up other users' screens with unnecessary messages.

Network Setup

This book takes into consideration that the reader is an end user. In addition, the text acquaints readers with the responsibilities and tasks required of an administrator. For training purposes, it is advisable to set up home directories for each user under a main directory called SYS : USERS. This will help the labs run consistently. Readers should have access to a NetWare 4.1 network and workstations that are running DOS locally. This book is set up to accommodate users who have earlier versions of DOS (except for the DELTREE, MSBACKUP, and MSD commands, which require version 6.0 or later). Chapter 2 provides a helpful review of frequently used DOS commands.

Acknowledgments

Networking is a highly technical and ever-changing field, thus writing this book was at times very difficult and required the assistance of many people. I wish to thank everyone who took part in helping this book to be written, edited, printed, and finally provided to the readers.

First of all, I thank my husband, Tito, for his constant support and patience. Second, thanks to my son, who served as an inspiration. It was during my maternity leave that I wrote the first draft for this book. I thank the many networking students who helped to pilot test the early drafts of the manuscript and gave much valuable feedback. I also thank all of the staff and faculty at Computer Learning Center for their support, input, and encouragement, and I especially thank Al Steuart for giving me the opportunity to teach networking. Special thanks go to John Epps for serving as a mentor and encouraging me to complete what I started. Thanks go to all the people at Prentice Hall, especially Hal Balmer, Charles Stewart, Steve Robb, and Debbie Yarnell for their dedication and professionalism in getting this book ready for the readers. I wish to also acknowledge Kathleen Lafferty at Roaring Mountain Editorial Services for her keen attention to detail and doing such a fine job on editing the book.

Finally, I thank the following reviewers for their insightful suggestions: Robert P. Diffenderfer, DeVry Institute of Technology; John Hilby, Perry Technical Institute; Jim Barlow, Computer Learning Center.

Technical Advisor

Very special thanks go to my technical advisor for this book, Marc A. Busch, Enterprise Certified NetWare Engineer/Certified NetWare Engineer/Certified NetWare Administrator. During the writing of this book he served as the vice president of the Orange County Network Professional Association and was lead CNE instructor at Computer Learning Center. Mr. Busch answered numerous networking questions and examined the manuscript's technical content.

CONTENTS

GETTING STARTED

I

Part I introduces basic networking concepts and presents a review of DOS commands encountered most often on the network.

CHAPTER ONE

LAN BASICS

INSPIRING MOMENT

Through the use of today's local area network (LAN), electronic mail software applications make writing interoffice memos easy. Most e-mail systems today also make it possible to send the same memo to a group of users. Some e-mail systems even keep a record of which users have actually opened the electronic message that was sent, so you know exactly the date and time that your memo was read. Managers, supervisors, and team leaders can use e-mail to inform team members of the objectives of the day. Instead of chasing people in the hallways, you can leave them mail. A computer can be set up to notify users when they log in that they have mail. (See Chapter 10.)

QUESTIONS FOR THOUGHT

Can you imagine not having to wait for the copy machine to work, and not having to unclog paper jams when photocopying memos for distribution? Can you imagine what an office would be like if "telephone tag" didn't exist anymore? Can you imagine holding a meeting where everyone shows up, or at least no one can use the excuse, "I didn't get the memo announcing the meeting"? Can you imagine having a department where all the workers know the objectives of the day and know exactly what they are supposed to be doing? How is all this possible?

CHALLENGE

Does your network have an electronic mail application installed? If so, ask your network administrator or other personnel how to use it. After bringing the e-mail menu up, it's usually straightforward and easy to use. With a little practice, you can send important messages to your associates.

OBJECTIVES

After finishing this chapter, you should be able to:

1. Define *local area network* and list the benefits involved in using a LAN.
2. Identify the key components of a LAN: a file server, a network operating system

(NOS), workstations, a local operating system (LOS), network interface cards (NICs), and cables.

3. Explain how a workstation attaches to the NetWare network and identify key files required.

4. Explain steps and files required for logging into the NDS tree.

5. Highlight common error messages associated with the attaching and logging in procedure.

6. Define *communication protocol* (access method) and list the popular types.

7. Define *topology* and list the popular types.

8. Discuss interconnectivity and its importance, and define common terms found in connecting different platforms together.

LOCAL AREA NETWORKS (LANs)

This chapter assumes that the Novell NetWare operating system is already installed on the file server, and that the LAN is up and running. (For help on installation, consult your Novell documentation manuals.)

Local area networks (LANs) allow computer users to share resources and communicate together, thus saving time and money and improving efficiency. Users share hardware resources such as printers, plotters, fax/modems, CD-ROMs, and storage devices. They share software applications for word processing, spreadsheet management, database management, desktop publishing, computer-aided design, and so forth. Perhaps the most common service is to share data such as customer, employee, or vendor databases.

Without a LAN environment, users constantly run back and forth physically from station to station. With a LAN, improved communication, through sending short messages, electronic mail (e-mail), faxes, and even files of information, leads to more informed workers who can make better decisions and accomplish more.

LAN is a way in which several computers can connect together in short proximity (normally within a building); share resources such as software, hardware, and data; and communicate together. The key word is *connectivity*; in a LAN, the personal computers are all connected together to share resources and communicate.

To provide access to a LAN and maintain security, accounts are created. Without an account, you cannot use a LAN. To set up accounts, you should have access to the ADMIN account or have been assigned ADMIN-equivalent privileges. In a class setting, this may not be possible. As a student, though, you can view many of the settings of your own account, which should give you an ample opportunity to learn. The only restriction is that you cannot change the settings.

LAN security is a prime reason for assigning trustee directory rights and for setting up accounts. With proper training and care in deciding who should gain access to various parts of software and data, you can set up and manage accounts to help the company or organization with controlling and sharing of the resources on the LAN.

The network administrator oversees the day-to-day operation of the network.

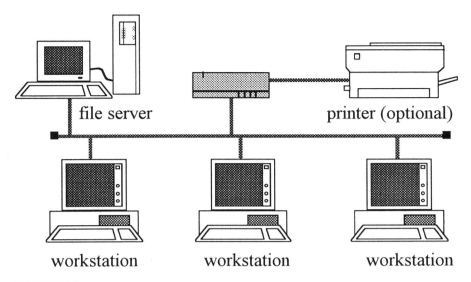

FIGURE 1.1
Key components of a local area network.

By setting up and managing user accounts, controlling security, creating comfortable work environments with tools such as menus and login scripts, making sure the printers are set up and working, maintaining server backups, and monitoring network performance, the network administrator makes sure that the users can work on the LAN easily and efficiently.

KEY COMPONENTS OF A LAN

LAN components include a file server, the network operating system (such as NOVELL NetWare), workstations, local operating systems for the workstations (such as DOS), network interface cards (NICs), cables, and possibly other hardware such as a printer or fax machine (see Figure 1.1). A basic knowledge of how these components function together makes working on the LAN more meaningful.

Component 1: File Server

The file server is the heart of the LAN (see Figure 1.2). Its purpose, as its name implies, is to serve the workstation files and other resources as requested. Keep in mind that the software and data that are to be shared among different users are normally stored on the file server's hard drive(s) or on a disk subsystem connected to the file server (a disk subsystem consists of a housing unit that holds additional drives). Because many users will share resources from the file server, it's important to keep it as secure as possible. Locking it in a closet is one way to secure it.

The file server is a personal computer that has a minimum of 8 megabytes

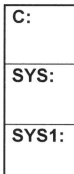

C: — DOS partition contains the C: drive

SYS: — NetWare partition contains volumes such as SYS: and SYS1:

SYS1:

FIGURE 1.2
Typical hard drive set up for a file server.

(MB) of random-access memory (RAM). Ideally, the file server will have upward of 16 MB of RAM. The hard drive of the file server will be shared by the users; therefore, it's wise to invest in as large of a hard drive as an organization can afford.

A dedicated file server constantly acts as a servant to the workstations by sharing resources and serving files. A nondedicated file server only acts as a servant part of the time; the rest of the time, it doubles as an ordinary workstation where a user can work on a software application. Novell NetWare 4.1x only runs in dedicated mode. Earlier versions of NetWare, such as release 2.15c, allow for nondedicated operation.

Component 2: Network Operating System (NOS)

Personal computers (PCs) speak the disk operating system (DOS) language, whereas the file server speaks or uses the network operating system (NOS) to operate and perform day-to-day functions or tasks. Novell NetWare is a common NOS. The file server is booted like any other PC; the hard drive itself is set up differently, however. The file server's hard drive has a minimum of two partitions or sections. One partition is referred to as a DOS partition, and it contains the files necessary for booting. It also contains SERVER.EXE, which, when executed, starts the network. (SERVER.EXE is normally found in a subdirectory called C:\NWSERVER.) The DOS partition contains divisions called drives such as C: and D:. The file server's other partition is known as a non-DOS NetWare partition. Rather than being called drives, the divisions of the NetWare partition are known as volumes, such as SYS: and SYS1:. When the file server is activated and the network is brought up by executing the SERVER.EXE file, the colon prompt (:) appears on the file server's screen. The colon prompt denotes that the file server is ready to receive keyboard instructions from the file server console and that it speaks NOS language, namely, Novell NetWare 4.1. (This is similar to having a C:\> prompt at the workstation indicating that the station is ready for instructions and that DOS is the local operating system.) Network drives, which are normally letters F: through Z:, are covered in more detail in Chapter 3.

Component 3: Workstations

The workstation is usually a personal computer on which a user logs in. Note that in a LAN environment, distributed processing rather than centralized processing is used. In a mainframe or midrange platform, the actual processing takes place at the main unit, not at each workstation. The stations are therefore often referred to as *dumb terminals* because they do not have central processing units (CPUs). In a LAN platform environment, however, the workstations do have CPUs and process their own work. Once software (or data) has been requested from the file server, it is loaded into the RAM of the workstation for the actual processing. Because the processing power is scattered among different workstations on the LAN, the term used is *distributed processing.* In a mainframe or midrange environment, however, because the processing is sent to one main place, the term used is *centralized,* or *shared, processing.* Because the file server's hard drive and/or disk subsystem may be shared by all users, some companies and organizations eliminate the drives on the workstation. Under such circumstances the network interface card (NIC) would contain a special chip known as a boot PROM (programmable read-only memory) for getting the workstation started. The boot PROM contains instructions to allow the workstation to boot, or get started. Some companies have workstations fully equipped with floppy drives, hard drives, and perhaps even tape drives. In such cases, the workstation would boot up by running instructions found in three special files on drive C:'s root directory: COMMAND.COM, IO.SYS, and MSDOS.SYS. With more recent versions of DOS, the workstation may even have a fourth boot-up file that controls file compression. If drive A: has a disk in it and the drive door is closed, then the system would try to find the three files required for booting in drive A: instead of in the hard drive C:. The booting or start-up process loads the local operating system (LOS) so that the workstation can function.

Component 4: Local Operating System (LOS)

To operate a personal computer, you must first start it using an operating system software such as DOS (disk operating system). The following DOS files are needed to boot your system: IO.SYS, MSDOS.SYS, and COMMAND.COM (see Figure 1.3). Note that IO.SYS and MSDOS.SYS do not appear in a normal directory listing because they are hidden. These three files collectively are often referred to as *system files.* The computer itself is just a machine; it needs software (instructions) to operate. Operating system software such as DOS provides the instructions needed for day-to-day operations. When referring to software or hardware items specifically for the workstation, the word *local* is used. In this discussion, booting and operating the workstations are the goals of the local operating system.

Network drives (F: through Z:) are discussed in Chapters 3 and 4. The first network drive is accessible only after the workstation attaches to the network. The user must log in to access the remaining drives. The running of network software

system files on disk (hard drive or floppy)	when the computer starts, these system files go to the computer's memory	the prompt appears on the screen

COMMAND.COM IO.SYS MSDOS.SYS	random access memory	C:\> = local drive F:\> = network drive

FIGURE 1.3

needed for attaching is normally initiated in the AUTOEXEC.BAT file. Everyday users are usually not aware of this because AUTOEXEC.BAT executes automatically.

Component 5: Network Interface Card (NIC)

Each computer on the LAN, including all workstations and the file server, must have an NIC (network interface card). An NIC is the hardware that allows the computer to receive and send messages. An NIC is sometimes referred to as an adapter. The NIC is controlled by a software program called a LAN driver. The LAN driver is normally provided by the NIC manufacturer. Novell provides a copy of some of the more standard LAN drivers; these come with the workstation installation software provided with your NOS.

Component 6: Cables or Media

Cables connect all the workstations and the file server together. There are various cabling systems available today. Some of the more well-known types are coaxial (base band and broad band), twisted pair (shielded and unshielded), and fiber-optic cables. The type of cable chosen depends on cost factors, electrical interference around the LAN, the experience of the person installing the cabling, and, in some cases, the topology, or cable layout, chosen.

Twisted pair cabling is fairly inexpensive and is easy to install, but it provides the least resistance to electrical interference. The most commonly expressed forms of twisted pair cabling are unshielded twisted pair (UTP) and shielded twisted pair (STP). STP provides some extra protection against electrical interference. Coaxial cabling is in the middle; it offers a fair amount of resistance to electrical interference, costs a little more than twisted pair, and is somewhat more difficult than twisted pair to install. Fiber-optic cabling is at the high end of the scale in terms of its ability to withstand electrical interference, its high cost, and the need for a highly skilled person to install it. Cabling is also referred to by some as media, because it is the media through which signals and pieces of software and data are sent.

WORKSTATION COMMUNICATIONS

First, a workstation must "attach" to the network before it's considered an "active" or "connected" station. With networks that run the Novell NetWare 3.x or 4.x NOS, this attaching process follows the networking industry's open data-link interface (ODI) method. That means that it's more flexible, allowing for a variety of workstations that may be logging in to the same network. Several files are used with the ODI method of attaching, as discussed below.

Key ODI Files

The four main ODI files for workstation communication are (1) the LSL.COM, or link support layer, (2) the NE2000.COM or other LAN driver, (3) the IPXODI communication protocol, or internetwork packet exchange open datalink interface, and (4) the VLM.EXE, or virtual loadable module and supporting file NET.CFG. These main ODI files, and others, are usually located in a directory called C:\NWCLIENT.

Link Support Layer (LSL) The link support layer, or LSL.COM, is a software program that, when executed, acts as a mediator or switchboard operater. This file is the first of the four key files to execute. Its purpose is to control or enforce "turn taking" by the LAN driver and the communication protocol. LSL determines whose turn it is to "speak."

LAN Driver The LAN driver is a software program that, when executed, controls the operation of the NIC. The LAN driver software program is supplied by the manufacturer of the NIC as part of the NIC package. Novell also supplies driver disks that contain some well-known LAN drivers. The file name for the LAN driver controlling the workstation NICs normally ends with an .EXE or .COM extension. The file name for the LAN driver controlling the file server's NIC normally ends with a .LAN extension. NE2000.COM is one of the most widely used LAN drivers supplied by Novell. (It's common for an NIC manufacturer to advertise its product as being NE2000 compatible.)

Communication Protocol The communication protocol, discussed later in this chapter, divides data into packets, assigns each data packet a source and destination address (corresponding to the sender and receiver), and controls the sending of packets along the network. In our examples, we refer to IPXODI, the communication protocol for DOS workstations on the network.

Virtual Loadable Module and NET.CFG The virtual loadable module, or

VLM.EXE, allows the workstation to attach to the file server (network). It also allows the workstation to request different types of services. Because the workstation normally runs DOS as its local operating system, VLM.EXE is also known as the DOS requestor. This module is no longer an ''all or nothing'' proposition; for instance, users can decide if printing is a needed service. When executed, VLM.EXE reads a configuration data file named NET.CFG. The NET.CFG file specifies which services the user would like. It also allows the user to customize different aspects relating to LSL, the LAN driver, and the communication protocol.

Other Files

Other files include the workstation's AUTOEXEC.BAT and CONFIG.SYS FILES, NET.CFG (network configuration file), and STARTNET.BAT (network batch file). For the most part, the workstation installation software that comes with Novell NetWare will automatically set up everything. It's still best, however, to understand what is going on in case changes are needed or something does not work correctly.

STARTNET.BAT   Below is an example of the STARTNET.BAT. This file is automatically put on the hard drive when the workstation installation software is executed. (The workstation installation lab is at the end of the chapter.)

```
SET NWLANGUAGE=ENGLISH
C:\NWCLIENT\LSL.COM
:DRIVER
C:\NWCLIENT\NE2000.COM
C:\NWCLIENT\IPXODI.COM
C:\NWCLIENT\VLM.EXE
F:\
LOGIN
```

The STARTNET.BAT file contains the commands needed to run the four key ODI files mentioned earlier. Inside the STARTNET.BAT file, the following lines are found:

    LSL

    NE2000

    IPXODI

    VLM

Once the STARTNET.BAT file is executed, the workstation should be attached to the network (assuming that cable problems or NIC hardware-level addressing conflicts do not exist). The order in which the command appears is very critical. If they are listed in a different order, the workstation will not attach to the network.

NET.CFG   Below is an example of the NET.CFG file. As with the STARTNET.-BAT, it is automatically added to the hard drive when the workstation installation program is executed. In this particular example, a Novell NE2000 NIC is installed in the user's workstation. Notice that the "FIRST NETWORK DRIVE" statement indicates that F: will be the first drive and that the prompt for logging in will be F:\>.

```
LINK SUPPORT
      BUFFERS 8 1514
      MEMPOOL 4096

LINK DRIVER NE2000
      PORT 300
      INT 3
      FRAME ETHERNET_802.3
      FRAME ETHERNET_802.2
      FRAME ETHERNET_II

PROTOCOL STACK IPX
      BIND NE2000

NetWare DOS Requester
      FIRST NETWORK DRIVE = F
      NETWARE PROTOCOL = NDS BIND
      name context="CONSULTANTS.ABC_CO"
```

CONFIG.SYS   CONFIG.SYS contains commands instructing the local operating system how to divide up the computer's RAM resources. By default, a PC is set up to have drive pointers ranging from A: to E:. The pointers are stored in RAM. If the workstation installation program has already been executed, the following line usually appears inside the CONFIG.SYS file to accommodate the need for additional drive pointers:

```
LASTDRIVE=Z
```

This extends RAM resources for having drive pointers ranging from A: to Z:.

AUTOEXEC.BAT   The AUTOEXEC.BAT file is normally located in the root directory of the C: drive (possibly the A: drive) at the workstation. Upon booting up the workstation, it is automatically executed. For network drives F: through Z: to be accessed, additional RAM resources must be allocated during the workstation's initial booting. As mentioned earlier, F: is usually the first network drive that users encounter. If the workstation installation program has already been executed, the following line normally appears inside the AUTOEXEC.BAT file:

```
@CALL C:\NWCLIENT\STARTNET.BAT
```

This instructs the local operating system to run a batch file called STARTNET.BAT located in the C:\NWCLIENT directory.

NETWARE DIRECTORY SERVICES (NDS) TREE

As mentioned earlier, one benefit of having a LAN is sharing of resources. With Novell NetWare 4.x, these resources are tracked in a global, distributed, hierarchical database known as Novell Directory Services (NDS). The NDS is actually a database that represents all the resources on the network in question.

When logging into the network, the user is actually logging into the NDS. The NDS also proves helpful for controlling security, addressed in Chapter 9.

The NDS is organized in an upside-down, treelike fashion with the "roots" of the tree located at the top. Off the root is normally found a container used for grouping and organization. There are different types of containers. If a company or organization is very large, doing business worldwide, then the type of container that attaches to the root is most likely a "country" container ("C="). For our examples, we will use a simple, medium-sized company. Therefore, our first container will be an "organization" container ("O="). For further clarity, we will divide our organization into departments, or "organizational unit" ("OU=") containers. The inside of each department's organizational unit containers will represent the actual resources. Resources may be a user, print queue, file server, volume, and so forth. Resources represented in this way are referred to as *leaves.*

Context

Before logging in, make sure the network operating system knows which organization container you are attempting to access and which organizational unit container you wish to log in to. This current location in the tree where you are is known as the *current context.* Check the current context by using the "cx" (context) command:

```
F:\>cx
```

It may be easier to go to the root first. If you did not get a reply message of "[root]," then use the "cx ." command to move down the tree. (*Note:* There is a space between the "cx" and the "."; if you do not use the space, you will get an error message saying that you issued a bad command.)

```
F:\>cx .
```

Note: Add one dot for each level you wish to move down.

Once at the root, specify your particular context. Keep in mind that the organization goes last. Remember, it's an upside-down tree.

```
F:\>cx .ou=acct .o=abc_co
```

or

```
F:\>cx .acct.abc_co
```

Notice that the second example uses a shortcut known as *typeless naming. Hint:* Once you figure out the right context and logging in procedure for your account, write it down. These notes will come in handy until you commit the steps to memory.

Now you're ready to log in.

LOGGING IN PROCESS

Once attached to the network, you are ready to log in. First, if the workstation screen still shows a C:\> prompt, change to a network prompt by keying in F: and pressing enter. (If F: is not the first available network drive, then press the appropriate letter corresponding to the first network drive.) At the F:\> prompt, key in the word LOGIN. (If the screen already shows "Enter your login name," your system has already been preprogrammed for this step).

```
F:\>LOGIN
Enter Your Login Name:
```

At this point, key in your login name, also referred to as an account name. The system will prompt you for your password. When you key in your password, notice that it does not appear on the screen. No one can see your password, not even the administrator. You can also enter the LOGIN command and your login name on the same line:

```
F:\>LOGIN SUPERMAN
Password:
```

COMMON ERROR MESSAGES ASSOCIATED WITH ATTACHING AND LOGGING IN

The first level of security on a Novell NetWare system is the login name and password level. A user may receive an error message when attempting to log in. Some key error messages associated with attaching and logging in to the network are discussed below.

"File Server Not Found" or "Invalid Drive Specification"

Most LAN troubleshooting problems are associated with cabling and connections. "File Server Not Found" or "Invalid Drive Specification" usually indicates that the workstation could not get a good connection to the network. If this happens, double check the cabling. Check the connection leading to the user's workstation and the connection leading from the workstation going toward the file server (this may be at a concentrator or hub). Make sure the cable is plugged in all the way. If this does not work, the cable may need replacing. Test the workstation with a cable known to work, or test the suspected bad cable using a cable-testing device. A whole row of stations getting the same error message usually indicates that the point at which the stations meet, the *hub* or *concentrator,* has a weak connection or that the power to the hub or concentrator is not turned on. If all the workstations connected to the same file server are getting the same error message, then check the *backbone* cabling (the main cable leading from the file server and going throughout the network). If the backbone is not the problem, perhaps the file server is down or has some other problem. Check the file server itself. If needed, call your network engineer to assist you.

"Access Denied" or "Intruder Detection Lockout"

"Access Denied" generally means that either your login name or password is keyed in incorrectly. Notice that the error message itself has a level of security to it. It doesn't tell you which is incorrect, your login name or your password. If the network administrator has the feature called "Intruder Detection" turned on, however, then the message "Access Denied" will change to "Intruder Detection Lockout" if the login name is correct and the wrong password has been entered more than the number of allowable attempts set by the administrator. The number of allowable attempts set by the administrator is referred to as login attempts allowed.

COMMUNICATION PROTOCOLS AND ACCESS METHODS

Protocols refer to the procedures or rules. For example, there are rules regulating how data packets are sent across the LAN. When a software application or data file is sent from the file server to the workstation, it must be sent in small pieces called data packets. The most popular protocols are carrier sense multiple access/collision detection (CSMA/CD), also known as contention; polling; and token passing.

Carrier Sense Multiple Access/Collision Detection (CSMA/CD) or Contention

The carrier sense multiple access/collision detection (CSMA/CD) protocol is commonly used with a bus topology. The workstation's NIC card must look to see if the channel (cable path) is busy before sending anything to the file server. If more than one workstation sends at the same time, and there is a "data collision," however, this is detected by the network, and the workstations' NICs will resend.

This procedure takes place behind the scenes; other than perhaps noticing slower sending or receiving, the user may be unaware of these events. On most systems, this happens at such a high rate of speed that it is doubtful the user will notice. The advantages of CSMA/CD are that it is straightforward to install, is cost effective, and has normally high throughput. The disadvantages are that time delays may occur in a busy LAN environment and that during busy traffic times bottlenecks may occur from several workstations sending at one time.

Collisions are common in CSMA/CD environments. They occur as traffic increases on the network, yet users continue operating as usual. When there is a crash, people sometimes refer to it as a collision.

Note: A collision and a crash differ in that a collision usually does not affect LAN operations, whereas with a crash, the entire LAN does not function (in other words, the LAN is down). Networks that use the CSMA/CD access method are often referred to as belonging to the "Ethernet" family.

Polling

With the polling protocol, more processing power on the part of the file server is required. The file server checks with each workstation, one by one, to see if there are any requests or commands that need processing. The star topology normally uses the polling protocol. The advantages of polling are that there is more control by the file server and that the amount of throughput is consistent. The disadvantage is that the file server's CPU has to work harder.

FIGURE 1.4
Bus topology.

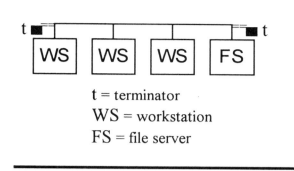

t = terminator
WS = workstation
FS = file server

Token Passing

In the token-passing protocol, a token is passed throughout the LAN from workstation to workstation. Imagine a small elevator going up and down between floors
in a tall building. There is only room for one passenger in this tiny elevator. If the
elevator is already occupied, however, the would-be next passenger can press a
button to indicate that he or she would like to ride next. After dropping off the
current passenger, the elevator would then go to the floor from which that next
request came. Similarly, on a network that uses token passing, the workstation
waits until an electronic box (signal) called a token comes around. If the electronic
token does not have any pending requests being processed, the station can put an
instruction, such as "retrieve a file," into the token. If the token is already full, the
workstation's NIC will simply tag the token to indicate that it needs to place an
instruction when available. The token passes between the workstation and the file
server. The file server carries out the instructions and relays the answer back to
the requesting workstation.

WORKING WITH CABLING

Topologies

Topology refers to how the cables are arranged, or the cable layout. Popular
topologies are bus, ring, star, mesh, and hybrid.

In a *bus topology* (see Figure 1.4), workstations are normally connected in a
straight line, one after the other. Each end of the line is capped off with a *terminator,*
one at either end; this marks the end of the bus segment.

In a *ring topology* (see Figure 1.5), workstations are connected in a circular
pattern with the file server also attached to the circle. The ends of the circle normally
connect to the file server.

In a *star topology* (see Figure 1.6), the file server is in the center and each
workstation connects to a box connected to the file server.

FIGURE 1.5
Ring topology.

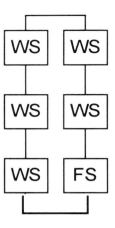

WS = workstation
FS = file server

In a *mesh topology* (Figure 1.7), each computer, including the file server, is connected together with cables. The connections are considered point to point.

In a *hybrid topology,* various topologies are integrated together to best meet the needs of the installation site.

Each topology has its advantages and disadvantages. The advantage of the bus and ring topologies is that they require less cabling than other methods; therefore, they are less expensive. Their disadvantage is that to add or remove workstations, someone must bring down the file server first. Thus, no one can use the

FIGURE 1.6
Star topology.

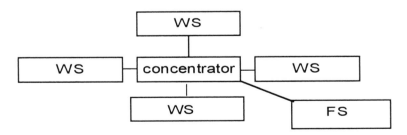

WS = workstation
concentrator = connection box
FS = workstation

FIGURE 1.7
Mesh topology.

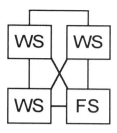

WS = workstation
FS = file server

LAN while this type of maintenance takes place. With star ring topologies, on the other hand, each of the workstations has its own cable; therefore, someone may add or remove workstations without taking down the file server. Their disadvantage is that the amount of cabling required is significantly more than with the bus or ring topologies; therefore, they are more expensive to use than other methods.

LAN VERSUS OTHER PLATFORMS

In a LAN environment, each workstation's CPU does its own work. This type of environment has traditionally been known as distributed or decentralized processing, which is different from a standard mainframe or midrange environment. For example, in a normal midrange environment, workstations do not process their own work. Programs are submitted from the workstations to a central location, commonly called a data center. The main CPU for this type of environment is shared among several workstations. This type of processing is referred to as centralized processing. The advantage to working in a LAN environment where decentralized processing occurs is that the user does not have to submit programs for processing; the programs are processed right at the user's station.

INTERCONNECTIVITY

Before LANS became popular, companies invested considerable money into personnel, hardware, and software resources for mainframe and midrange computers. Many companies are still buying these larger-size computers. A need has arisen for interconnecting midrange, mainframes, and PCs found together on a LAN. Thus the term *interconnectivity* is used.

In general, interconnectivity means the connecting of computers on more than one platform. Platforms are characterized as consisting of different kinds of computers running under different operating systems. This section discusses several common terms associated with interconnectivity.

The term *downsizing* became very popular in the early 1990s as companies cut their budgets and reduced their work forces. And downsizing made LANs more popular. Mainframes, with all their workstations, were generally more expensive to buy and maintain than a LAN system consisting of PCs. Improved speed and performance of CPU chips also influenced the move toward LANs. Hard drives capable of storing 1 gigabyte (GB) of data also have influenced buying decisions.

Instead of having to buy both workstations for LANs and dumb terminals for the mainframe or midrange platforms, companies are now using gateways and terminal emulation. Through this technology, PCs can communicate both to the file server on the LAN and to the other platform (mainframe or midrange), thus saving a company or organization the cost of the dumb terminal and the space needed for additional equipment. Gateways have an advantage over terminal emulation and represent a newer technology. With a gateway, any workstation already on the LAN can communicate with the other platform. With terminal emulation, each workstation must have its own special emulation card and appropriate software, as well as a separate cable connecting it to the other platform.

Bridge

A bridge is a method of using special hardware and software to allow two LANs to connect together. Two major types of bridges exist, internal and external. With internal bridging, one file server contains two NICs. Each NIC connects to a separate LAN. With external bridging, a dedicated PC connected to the backbone contains two NICs, each connected to a separate file server and associated LAN, using special Novell bridging software to connect the two separate LANs.

Gateway

A gateway is a method of using special hardware and software to connect dissimilar platforms, such as a LAN and a mainframe or midrange computer.

Terminal Emulation

Terminal emulation consists of a special computer card and software that allows a PC to act like a dumb terminal for purposes of communicating to the host computer in a centralized processing–type platform.

Host and Client

In a bridge or gateway environment, the host is the platform that provides requested data and the client is the platform that receives the data. For example, if your workstation (hooked up to the LAN) makes a request through the gateway for some customer data records stored on the mainframe, the LAN then serves as the client and the mainframe as the host.

SUMMARY

A LAN consists of different components that work together to allow for the sharing of data and software and hardware resources and to facilitate communication. Putting these components together first requires deciding on the topology or layout of cables (bus, ring, star, or hybrid), cabling type (twisted pair, coaxial, or fiber-optic cables), the protocol or sending procedures (polling, CSMA/CD, or token passing), the local operating system (such as DOS), and the network operating system (such as Novell NetWare 4.x). Making these decisions requires both practice and training. The lab at the end of this chapter takes a first-hand look at workstation installation and logging in to the network.

EXERCISES

1. Define the following:
   (a) LAN
   (b) file server
   (c) workstation
   (d) NIC
   (e) media
   (f) local operating system
   (g) topology
   (h) protocol
   (i) terminal emulation
   (j) bridge
   (k) gateway
   (l) downsizing
   (m) system files
2. What do the following stand for?
   (a) LAN
   (b) ODI
   (c) NIC
   (d) NOS
   (e) LOS
   (f) LSL
   (g) VLM
   (h) UTP
   (i) STP
   (j) CSMA/CD

3. List the components making up a LAN.

4. Name four topologies and list the advantages and disadvantages of each.

5. Name three protocols and list the advantages and disadvantages of each.

6. Fill in the blank with the instruction line found in the CONFIG.SYS file that instructs the local operating system to allow for drive pointers A: through Z:.

---

7. Fill in the blank with the command line found in the AUTOEXEC.BAT file that instructs the local operating system to run the STARTNET.BAT batch file.

---

8. What is the name of the directory that holds the workstation ODI files?

9. Which file is called by AUTOEXEC.BAT, and where is it located?

10. List the four key ODI files called by STARTNET.BAT. (Make sure to list them in the correct sequence.) What is the purpose of each?

11. What is the name of the configuration data file associated with the DOS requestor?

12. What is the purpose of LOGIN.EXE?

13. What are some reasons for having a LAN?

14. Why is it important to log out when leaving your workstation unattended?

15. Your company is very concerned about having to add or delete workstations periodically throughout the day and has asked you to recommend the cabling type and the topology for the LAN. The cost of cable is very expensive in your area. What do you recommend and why?

16. You work for a company that is surrounded by high-power electrical lines. Throughout the company, computer files have been damaged, and engineers suspect that this may be the result of having the wrong cable type installed. What do you recommend, and why do you think the engineers came to the conclusion mentioned?

17. Prepare a floppy disk that will allow you to boot your computer and then attach to the server. (*Caution:* For security reasons, it is not advisable to include your password on your disk.)

LAB 1A

Workstation installations are the steps required to set up a PC as a network workstation. Once this has been done, the new workstation can then be recognized by the network, and users can log in. In this particular lab, you will go through the workstation installation process.

1. Sit at a station that is already set up with both MS-DOS and MS-WINDOWS. This lab assumes that your workstation has a hard drive C: and at least one 3⁄₀ inch floppy disk drive. It also assumes that you have the three workstation installation disks.

2. Boot your computer (do not log in). Go to the prompt associated with the 3⁄₀ inch floppy drive.

```
C:\>B:
B:\>
```

3. Put the disk labeled ''WS_DOS1'' into the drive.

4. Type ''install.''

    `B:\>`**`INSTALL`**

5. The screen should now come up with many setting questions. For this lab, use all the defaults until you get to screen step 4, asking you to install a LAN driver. Highlight the selection and press ''enter.'' Fill in the following table with the questions asked for each step listed on the screen:

Step 1.
Step 2.
Step 3.
Step 4.
Step 5.

6. You are now prompted to put in the LAN driver disk. Take out the WS_DOS1 disk and insert the disk associated with the driver. You may use the LAN driver disk provided by the NIC manufacturer or the one provided by Novell. Press ''enter'' when ready.

7. A list of available LAN drivers should now appear on your screen. The list does not actually contain the file names for the drivers, but rather a descriptive name. Pick the descriptive name most closely associated with your NIC. Document your selection: What type of NIC do you have? Which descriptive name did you choose?

8. Next, your screen should display configuration information for that particular driver file. At this point, you may choose to take the defaults or check the NIC itself for the actual setting information. Write down the setting information that appeared after you made your selection:

Write down any changes that you made to the settings:

```
┌─────────────────────────────────────────────────────────────┐
│                                                             │
├─────────────────────────────────────────────────────────────┤
│                                                             │
├─────────────────────────────────────────────────────────────┤
│                                                             │
│                                                             │
└─────────────────────────────────────────────────────────────┘
```

9. Press "escape" to continue and choose step 5 from the screen. This is the actual installation step.
10. Your next prompt is to insert the three installation disks, one at a time. Some disks may be needed more than once.
11. Once the installation is complete, the system will need rebooting. Do that when the message for booting appears on your screen. You have just completed a workstation installation.

LAB 1B

In this lab, you will investigate the results of your workstation installation. You will learn what changes were made to the AUTOEXEC.BAT and CONFIG.SYS files. You will also look at the ODI directory C:\NWCLIENT and discover the contents of the most important ODI-related files.

1. Go to the root directory of the C: drive and view the CONFIG.SYS file:

   ```
   C:\>TYPE CONFIG.SYS
   LASTDRIVE = _____ (fill in the blank)
   ```

2. From the root directory of the C: drive, view the contents of the AUTOEXEC. BAT file:

   ```
   C:\>TYPE AUTOEXEC.BAT
   @CALL_____ (fill in the blank)
   ```

3. Look at your answer on the "@CALL_____." What is the name of the subdirectory being referenced? What is the name of the file being referenced?
4. The subdirectory is called C:\NWCLIENT. Change to that directory now. Use the change directory (CD) command from DOS:

   ```
   C:\>CD NWCLIENT
   C:\NWCLIENT>
   ```

5. View the contents of the directory:

   ```
   C:\NWCLIENT>DIR/P
   ```

6. The file referenced in the AUTOEXEC.BAT file is called STARTNET.BAT. View this file:

```
C:\NWCLIENT>TYPE STARTNET.BAT
```

Write down the contents of the file. This may come in handy later.

STARTNET.BAT (Contents)

7. There are four key files called by STARTNET.BAT: the link support layer, LAN driver, communication protocol, and the DOS requestor. Complete the table below with the file names for your particular setup. (*Note:* The four files listed in the chart must be run in that particular order.)

ODI Section Heading	File Name
Link Support Layer	
LAN Driver	
Communication Protocol	
DOS Requestor	

8. When the DOS requestor (VLM.EXE) is executed, an associated configuration data file is also read. The name of the file is NET.CFG. View that file now:

```
C:\NWCLIENT>TYPE NET.CFG
```

Note: If there are too many lines to fit on your screen, add ¦MORE to your TYPE command. This will make the computer pause when the screen is full. Press "enter" for the next screen. Write down the contents of the NET.CFG file. This list may come in handy later.

9. Your NET.CFG file may reference virtual loadable modules (VLMs); these are also located in the C:\NWCLIENT directory. View the directory once more and see if you can now find all the files mentioned. Complete this checklist:

	STARTNET.BAT
	LSL (link support layer)
	NE2000 or other LAN driver
	IPXODI (communication protocol)
	VLM (virtual loadable module - DOS Requestor
	NET.CFG (associated configuration data file.)
	*.VLM (all the VLM files referenced by the NET.CFG file)
	any others?

LAB 1C

In Lab 1A, you explored workstation installation. Now that your workstation is set up, you are ready to log in. In this lab, you will practice logging in and out of the system. This lab assumes that the workstation installation has already been done.

1. Boot your workstation.
2. Change to the F:\> prompt if you are not already there:

```
C:\>F:
F:\>
```

3. Key in the word "login":

```
F:\>LOGIN
```

Note: If your screen already reads "enter your login name," do not type the word "login." The administrator for the LAN on which you are working has already preprogrammed this step for you.

4. The system should prompt you for your login name. Key it in at this time:

```
F:\>LOGIN
Enter Login Name: USER01
```

5. The prompt for your password is next. Key it in at this time:

```
F:\>LOGIN
Enter Login Name: USER01
Password:
```

Note: No one can see your current password, not even the **administrator. If you were not prompted for a password, check with the person who issued your login name.** It's possible that your account was set up not to require a password.

6. Always remember to log out when you are finished. Practice that now: type "logout."

7. Now, log in using the shortcut method: key in the word "login" and your login name on the same line and press "enter." The system will then ask for your password.

```
F:\>LOGIN USER01
Password:
```

CHAPTER TWO

DOS REVIEW

INSPIRING MOMENT

Many users log on to the network that you manage daily. Recently, you've noticed that many users have difficulty managing their workstations at a local level. You are constantly assisting users with copying files, managing them, and creating directories. You often spend hours just trying to fix problems associated with mistakes. Sometimes the workstations fail to boot up (start) properly. Also, you notice that users in general are not aware of the importance of making backups.

QUESTIONS FOR THOUGHT

Do you think that users should be exposed to a short training seminar in the use of DOS commands? If so, which commands would you include? How strong is your own knowledge of DOS? Are you comfortable managing files and directories in a DOS environment? What can you do to improve any weaknesses you or the users have in this area?

CHALLENGE

Read through this chapter and understand how each command works, but don't stop there. Learning the key DOS commands is not enough. Experiment, explore, and practice using each command. If you find that users need help in this area, hold a seminar to introduce them to the commands, or produce a handbook where you explain the various commands in your own words. Also, many good software tutors exist in this area; consider using one.

OBJECTIVES

After finishing this chapter, you should be able to:

1. Identify commonly used internal and external DOS commands and distinguish among them.

2. Manage files by creating, viewing, editing, erasing, changing attributes, and printing them.

3. Manage subdirectories by creating directories, performing directory searches, moving around in the system, performing routine backups, and removing directories.

4. Initialize a floppy disk and turn it into a system boot disk.

5. Use the PATH command to instruct the local operating system where to look for executable files.

6. Demonstrate the use of the DOS wild cards ? and *.

7. Use the DOS editor to create and edit files.

INTRODUCTION

A good working knowledge of the disk operating system (DOS) is essential before launching an exploration of networking. This chapter is a brief review of some of the commands and concepts of DOS.

DOS has two parts, internal and external. Those commands that may be performed once the computer has been booted up (without having to access a DOS subdirectory or DOS disk) are referred to as internal commands. External DOS commands are programs.

INTERNAL DOS COMMANDS

The following are commonly used internal DOS commands:

DIR
COPY
TIME
DATE
CLS
TYPE
ERASE
MD
CD
RD
PATH

DIR, COPY, ERASE, and TYPE

The DIR, COPY, ERASE, and TYPE commands allow users to manage and work with files located on storage devices found at the workstation or on the network. (The user must be granted permission to use network storage devices. This is discussed in Chapter 8.) The DIR, COPY, and ERASE commands may look different with the addition of the wild cards ? and *.

DIR *.EXE This command shows a directory of all files with the extension of .EXE (executable files).

DIR TEST?.BAT This command shows a directory of all files with the first four letters "TEST." The next, or fifth, character can be anything, and the extension ends with .BAT (batch files).

DIR TEST?.* This command shows a directory of all files with the first four letters "TEST." The next, or fifth, character can be anything, and the extension ends with anything.

COPY *.* B: This command copies all files from the current directory to the B: drive.

COPY C:\DATA\WPDATA\SJONES.LTR B: This command copies a file called SJONES.LTR that is currently in a subsubdirectory on the C: drive C:\DATA\WPDATA and puts the copy in the B: drive. Normally, subsubdirectories are just called subdirectories.

ERASE *.* This command erases all files from the current directory.

ERASE C:\DATA\WPDATA*.TXT This command erases all files from the C:\DATA\WPDATA subdirectory that end with the extension .TXT (text files).

TYPE

TYPE C:\DATA\WPDATA\SJONES.LTR >PRN This command simply instructs the computer to print the contents of the file called SJONES.LTR that is located in the subdirectory C:\DATA\WPDATA. The >PRN pipe option is used to redirect output to the printer. You can also use >PRN on other commands that give an output to the screen such as DIR >PRN. If you just want to see the work on the screen, simply leave off >PRN. If you are going to use the >PRN option in a LAN environment, that option is normally accompanied by the CAPTURE NetWare command (discussed in Chapter 6). Your LAN administrator can preprogram the CAPTURE command for you for now.

TIME, DATE, and CLS

The following internal commands cover basics of computer use.

TIME This command simply lets you see the current time setting and change it as needed. Note that the computer time is in military format; therefore, 1:00 P.M. is entered as 13:00. (You do not start over counting until you reach midnight, or 24:00.)

DATE This command allows you to change the current date on your computer. Many computers have built-in computer clocks, so the use of this command is not always necessary. Sometimes, however, it is needed to fool the computer into thinking that today is either an earlier or later date than it actually is. Changing the date becomes necessary when working report printing programs that rely on the system date. For example, when sending a mailing to 100 customers, you might want to have the letters dated next Monday to allow time to finish the in-house processing and would change the date accordingly.

CLS   This command simply allows you to clear the screen. This is handy when you want to erase whatever is on your screen quickly.

Make Directory (MD)

The following examples illustrate how the make directory (MD) command is used to create directories and subdirectories.

MD REPORTS   This command makes a subdirectory inside the current directory and calls it REPORTS. *Note:* Because no drive name or backslash is given, the subdirectory is made inside the current directory.

MD \REPORTS   This command makes a subdirectory from the current default drive. The slash indicates an immediate subdirectory off the root directory.

MD D:\REPORTS   This command specifically requests the computer to make a subdirectory in drive D:, right off the root, and call it REPORTS.

MD D:\REPORTS\NEWS   This command makes a subdirectory called D:\REPORTS\NEWS. The subdirectory D:\REPORTS must have already been created for this command to work properly; otherwise, you will get an error message.

Change Directory (CD)

The following examples illustrate how the change directory (CD) command is used to move to a different subdirectory or to move all the way back to the root directory of the drive. If the prompt on the screen reads C:\>, the local operating system is currently pointing to (looking at) the root directory or the C: drive.

CD   This command instructs the computer to change to the root directory in the current drive.

CD REPORTS   This command instructs the computer to change to the subdirectory REPORTS that is inside the current directory.

CD \REPORTS   This command instructs the computer to change to the subdirectory REPORTS that is off the root directory of the current drive.

CD D:\REPORTS   This command instructs the computer to change to the directory D:\REPORTS. (Be careful how you interpret this command.)

Remove Directory (RD)

The following examples illustrate how the remove directory (RD) command is used to get rid of unwanted subdirectories.

RD REPORTS   This command removes a subdirectory from inside the current directory. The subdirectory removed was called REPORTS. Because no drive name or backslash is given, the subdirectory is removed from inside the current directory (if it exists). The subdirectory REPORT must not contain any files or other subdirectories inside or an error message will appear on the screen and the subdirectory will not be removed.

RD \REPORTS   This command removes a subdirectory from the current default drive. The slash indicates an immediate subdirectory off the root directory. As with the prior example, the subdirectory REPORT must not contain any files or subdirectories inside or an error message will appear on the screen and the subdirectory will not be removed.

RD D:\REPORTS   This command specifically requests the computer to remove a subdirectory in drive D:, right off the root. The subdirectory removed was called REPORTS, given that it contained no other files or subdirectories inside.

PATH

The PATH command can help decrease the chances of receiving error messages by assisting the LOS and NOS in finding executable files. This command is discussed in more detail in Chapter 4.

PATH C:\;C:\DOS;C:\BATCH   If you issue an instruction to the computer to run an executable file (.EXE or .COM) or a batch file (.BAT) and the file name is not found, this command tells the computer to look elsewhere for it before giving an error message. In this case, the computer would first look in the root directory C: for the requested file. If it is not found there, the computer will look in the subdirectory C:\DOS. If it still is not found, the computer will look in the subdirectory C:\BATCH. If it still is not found, the computer will then display an error message.

EXTERNAL DOS COMMANDS

The word *commands* in referring to external DOS commands is a little deceiving. Actually, the external part of DOS is made up of programs. But the ease in using the programs leads many, if not most, people to call them commands.

The external part of DOS is not loaded into random-access memory (RAM) when you boot your computer. Unlike the internal part of DOS, the individual programs are loaded into RAM off your DOS subdirectory or DOS floppy disk on an as needed basis, whenever you decide to run an external DOS program.

Several programs make up external DOS, such as the following:

ATTRIB
BACKUP
CHKDSK
COMP
DISKCOPY
EDIT
EDLIN
FDISK
FORMAT
GRAPHICS
LABEL
MIRROR
MODE
RESTORE
SYS
TREE
UNDELETE
UNFORMAT
XCOPY

Some of these commands are discussed below.

ATTRIB

ATTRIB allows a user to view or modify characteristics of one or more files. These file characteristics are called attributes; attributes are also known as flags. The ATTRIB command is used to view and turn the different attribute flags on and off. Two of the most commonly used attributes, read only and hidden, are illustrated in this section. An additional attribute, archive needed, is discussed in the backup section.

The ATTRIB command is used to flag files located on the workstation's floppy and hard drive(s), but it is not used for files located on network drives controlled by the file server. To flag files located on a network drive controlled by the file server, use the NetWare command FLAG, which is discussed in Chapter 6.

*ATTRIB +H *.EXE*   This command instructs the computer to hide all the files in the current subdirectory that end with .EXE.

*ATTRIB +R *.TXT*   This command instructs the computer to allow the files to be read but not modified.

ATTRIB +H /S   This command instructs the computer to hide all files in all subdirectories under the current directory.

ATTRIB −H *.EXE   This command removes the hide attribute that was applied earlier (the minus sign reverses the operation).

ATTRIB   The command ATTRIB by itself will list the attributes of all the files in the current directory.

BACKUP and MSBACKUP

It's important to have backups of your directories and files. Hard drives have been known to crash occasionally, computer viruses have been known to invade and destroy or damage files, and users have been known to accidentally erase or unwantingly change file contents. BACKUP (for MS-DOS version 5.0 and prior) and MSBACKUP (for MS-DOS versions 6.x) allow users to take preventative measures by securing a backup copy of their files.

MSBACKUP (for MS DOS version 6.x)   The MSBACKUP command instructs the local operating system to run the Microsoft backup program and bring up the menu for it. These are the steps for menu selections when making backups.

Step 1   Getting into backup:

MSBACKUP	Go to Microsoft backup
Alt b	Select Backup

Step 2   Indicate which files are going to be backed up:

Alt k	Backup From
⇓	Press arrow down to select the drive letter corresponding to where your files are currently located. Press "enter."
⇓ Alt n	Highlight a directory or file that you want to back up, and hold down Alt and press n for its inclusion.
Alt e	Alt e allows you to edit your list of selected files for backup. Tab over to OK when done and press "enter."

Repeat the two steps, ⇓ Alt n and Alt e, until all directories and files to be backed up have been selected.

Step 3   Select the type of backup desired:

Alt y	Backup Type Choose from the following:

Alt f	Full
Alt I	Incremental
Alt d	Differential

The local operating system places (or turns on) an attribute of "archive needed" to a file when the file is modified or newly created. The archive needed attribute is treated as a flag used to control the backup process, depending on which backup type (listed above) is selected.

If the full backup type is selected, all the selected files, even if the archive needed flag is not turned on, are backed up. Once the backup is completed, the archive needed flags, if they exist, are removed. This is the most common backup type.

If the incremental backup type is selected, the selected files are only backed up if the archive needed flag is on. Once the backup is completed, the archive needed flags are removed.

If the differential backup type is selected, the selected files are only backed up if the archive needed flag is on, just as in incremental backups. Once the backup is completed, however, the archive needed flags are not removed. Some data-processing professionals use this option for daily backups because they like a complete backup of all changes at the end of the week. The incremental backup type is used at the end of the week to ensure that the archive needed flags are removed.

Step 4   Specify where the backups are to go:

Alt a	"Select Backup To" (you choose where to place the backups)
Alt a (floppy drive)	Select your particular floppy drive (press "enter" to confirm)
(floppy drive) or	
Alt d	"MS-DOS Drive and Path" (press "enter" to confirm)
(hard drive path)	Enter the path for your hard drive. For example, [D:\BACKUP . . . .]

Step 5   Include any special options desired:

Alt o   Options
There are a variety of special settings available. We will accept the defaults; press "enter" to continue.

Step 6   Start the backup process:

Alt s   Start Backup
The backup should proceed. If it does not allow you to select start backup, either you skipped a step or you chose incremental or differential backup type and no archive needed attributes were found on the files selected.

Step 7   Close the backup menu screen:

Alt q   Quit

Step 8   Save the backup settings:

Alt f   File

Alt a   Save Setup As
Enter a file name such as YOURNAME.SET and press "enter" to confirm.

Step 9   Exit Microsoft Backup

Alt f   File

Alt x   Exit

BACKUP C:*.* A: /S /L   This backup command will instruct the computer to back up all files in the C: drive. The A: means that the A: drive is the target.

Delete Tree (DELTREE)

The delete tree command (DELTREE) can be best compared to a tree trimmer. When a tree trimmer cuts off a tree branch, any attached smaller branches get discarded also. Similarly, when the local operating system executes the DELTREE program, any subdirectories inside the directory in question are removed.

DELTREE C:\TEMP   This command deletes the subdirectory called C:\TEMP along with any subdirectories or files that are located inside.

EDIT

The DOS EDIT program is actually referred to as the DOS editor. It allows an opportunity to create text files, batch files, and so forth. It is not as sophisticated as a word processor, because it was not designed for creating reports and other business type documents. The DOS editor is better used for viewing, creating, and editing files used by the local operating system or by NOS.

To use EDIT follow these steps.

Step 1   Verify the PATH: Because EDIT is a DOS program, it resides in the DOS directory. Verify that the DOS directory is being referenced in the PATH command:

```
C:\>PATH
```

The DOS directory path should be listed:

```
PATH = C:\;C:\DOS;C:\WINDOWS;C:\NWCLIENT
```

Step 2   Run the EDIT program and indicate the file name:

```
C:\>EDIT A:\MYTEST.BAT
```

Step 3   Key in the contents for the file in the EDIT entry screen (called the editor):

REM *****Sample batch file for changing the time and date*****

@ECHO OFF

TIME

DATE

CLS

Step 4   Exit and save your work:

Hold down Alt and press "F" for file.

Press "X" for exit.

Confirm that you want to save changes.

Step 5   Test your work:

View it: `C:\>TYPE A:\MYTEST.BAT`

Print it: `C:\>TYPE A:\MYTEST.BAT`

Run it: `C:\>A:\MYTEST.BAT`   (Do this step only if applicable.)

FORMAT   The FORMAT program initializes a new disk for saving work. The FORMAT command sets up the directory entry table (DET), defines the tracks (concentric circles) and sectors (segments of tracks), and checks for bad spots on the disk. Disks usually come preformatted.

The FORMAT A: command initializes the floppy disk in drive A: for the storing of files. The FORMAT A: /S command initializes the floppy disk in drive A: for the storing of files. It also transfers system files to the disk, making it a bootable.

Once the format operation and system file transfer process is complete, the floppy disk can be used to boot the computer. It's a good idea to make a floppy bootable disk and keep it stored in a safe place in case the boot files on the hard drive become damaged.

MSD Microsoft Diagnostics   Sometimes error messages alert the user that the operating system could not find a particular hardware device, such as a mouse, an NIC, or a printer. MSD is useful in accessing which hardware devices the system is recognizing and how such devices are being referenced.

MSD   This command brings up a menu-oriented screen that allows you to view hardware and memory configurations for a particular workstation.

SUMMARY

This chapter reviewed basic internal and external DOS commands. If you want to specialize in networking, you must become comfortable with DOS or whatever operating system is going to be accessed. If you know how to manage files and directories, the workstations for whose operation you are responsible should experience few problems and run more smoothly.

EXERCISES

1. Define the following:

(a) internal DOS

(b) external DOS

     (c) computer time (military time)

     (d) path

     (e) root directory

2. What happens when >PRN is added to the end of a TYPE command?
3. Which DOS commands are commonly used to manage and work with files?
4. Which DOS commands are commonly used to manage and work with directories?
5. To view the names of the files located on the A: drive, what command would you enter?
6. To copy a file called PROJECT1.TXT currently located in the path C:\LAN and store the new copy in the root directory of A:, what command should you enter?
7. To create a subdirectory on the A: drive called WORK, what command should you enter?
8. You changed your mind after question 7 and now wish to move PROJECT1.TXT from the root directory of the A: drive and place it in the newly created directory called WORK. What commands can you use to accomplish this?
9. How would you create the following directory tree structure?

```
                    Daisies
C:\Flowers————————Tulips          Miniature
                    Marigolds————————Regular
                                      Giant
```

10. If you key in the command DELTREE A:\MARIGOLDS, what are the results?
11. To hide the PROJECT1.TXT file currently in the WORK subdirectory on the A: drive, what command should you use?
12. Explain the benefit of using the PATH command.
13. Explain the difference among full, differential, and incremental backups.
14. Why are backups important?

LAB 2

Part 1   Using DOS at the Workstation Level

This lab allows you to explore uses for DOS at your own workstation. The more you practice, the more comfortable you will become with DOS. After completing this lab, you should have an understanding of how to initialize a floppy disk, copy files to it, create new files in subdirectories, edit an AUTOEXEC.BAT, and print.

1. Use the DIR command to view the directories on your workstation's hard drive:

```
C:\>DIR/P
```

Write down the path needed to access your DOS directory.

2. Display all the files located in the root directory of drive C: that end with the .BAT extension:

`C:\>`**DIR *.BAT**

3. Display the contents of your computer's AUTOEXEC.BAT file:

`C:\>`**TYPE AUTOEXEC.BAT**

Do you see the PATH command listed? Does it reference the DOS subdirectory as you indicated in your answer to step 1?

4. Format a new floppy disk for saving your work. Also make it bootable:

`C:\>`**FORMAT A:/S**

5. Make a subdirectory on drive A: and call it NOTES:

`C:\>`**MD A:\NOTES**

6. Use the DOS EDIT program to create a short text file:

`C:\>`**EDIT A:\NOTES\INTDOS.TXT**

Key in your thoughts about internal DOS and enter a list of the internal DOS commands discussed in Chapter 1.

Exit the EDIT program by holding down Alt and pressing "F" for file, then press "X" for exit. Confirm that you want to save changes.

7. Copy the AUTOEXEC.BAT and CONFIG.SYS files to your floppy disk:

`C:\>`**COPY AUTOEXEC.BAT A:**
`C:\>`**COPY CONFIG.SYS A:**

8. With your floppy disk still in the computer, reboot your computer. Your computer should be booting from the files in drive A:. To test this, modify the AUTOEXEC. BAT file located on the A: drive to display your notes:

`C:\>`**EDIT A:\AUTOEXEC.BAT**

Make sure you specify A:\ or you will be editing the AUTOEXEC.BAT on drive C: instead. Add this line to the bottom of the AUTOEXEC.BAT file:

TYPE A:\NOTES\INTDOS.TXT

If the printer is available, key the line in as follows:

TYPE A:\NOTES\INTDOS.TXT>PRN

Reboot your computer to test your changes. If all the steps were done correctly, your workstation should boot up from the floppy disk in drive A:. It then should proceed to run your newly edited AUTOEXEC.BAT, which displays your notes and prints them.

Part 2 Using DOS Commands on the Network

In this lab, you explore how DOS commands can also be used on the network. As you will soon discover, the commands work in the same way, with two exceptions: (1) The drive letters correspond to network drives, and (2) you must have been granted permission to use the files and directories on the network.

1. Log in following the steps used in the login lab found in Chapter 1.
2. At the F:\> prompt, view the names of the directories found on the network:

   F:\>**DIR/P**

3. Do you see the subdirectory called PUBLIC listed in the directory? (If not, see notes below for additional instructions.) Change to the PUBLIC directory:

   F:\>**CD PUBLIC**

4. Your prompt should now show that you are at the PUBLIC directory. Once again view the directory:

   F:\PUBLIC>**DIR/P**

5. You explored several DOS commands in this chapter; let's see which ones will work here. Try to create a new file:

   F:\PUBLIC>**EDIT NEWFILE.TXT**

   Type in a short text such as your name. Exit and save your work. Oops! You have not been granted permission to add new files to the PUBLIC directory.

   The PUBLIC directory, although accessible to everyone on the LAN, has security applied to it that prevents you from altering or adding to the contents of the subdirectory. This is discussed more in Chapter 8. DOS commands do work on the network, however, provided that you have been granted permission to work with the files and directories in the way you are attempting.

6. To further illustrate that you can use DOS commands while on the network, explore the copy command. Key in the following command:

   F:\PUBLIC>**COPY LOGOUT.EXE A:**

   You just instructed the computer to copy the file LOGOUT.EXE from the PUBLIC directory to your floppy drive.
        Verify that the copy command was successful:

   F:\PUBLIC>**DIR A:\LOGOUT.EXE**

   The file name LOGOUT.EXE should appear on your screen. (If the system just logged you out when you tried, log back in and try again. Most likely you forgot to type DIR before the word LOGOUT.)
        You really do not need the LOGOUT.EXE file on your floppy disk; you can erase it from the floppy disk now:

   F:\PUBLIC>**ERASE A:\LOGOUT.EXE**

If you accidentally forgot to put A:\ in keying in the command, you should receive an error message because you do not have permission to erase the original LOGOUT.EXE located in the PUBLIC directory. (If you did have permission, and you accidentally deleted LOGOUT.EXE from the PUBLIC directory, notify the LAN administrator for your network immediately.)

In this lab, you saw that several DOS commands can be used on the network. You will get the opportunity to enter and work with more DOS commands on the network in Chapter 3's lab.

MANAGING DIRECTORIES AND FILES

Part II helps users organize files and directories and locate them on the network.

CHAPTER THREE

DIRECTORY MANAGEMENT

INSPIRING MOMENT

Congratulations on your new position! You now work for a company that has an average-size network consisting of somewhere between 30 and 100 users, a handful of printers, and a file server or two. But the people normally available to answer questions are out of the office all week, attending a networking conference. In this networking environment, you sometimes feel lost and are not sure of the location of different directories. You do not know how much access you have to various directories. Once logged into the network, you find that moving around in the system takes time. When the change directory (CD) command is entered to a different directory, the paths are very long and require much typing.

QUESTIONS FOR THOUGHT

What should you do? How do you feel? If you have users for whom you are also responsible, what should you do? How do you think they feel?

CHALLENGE

Read this chapter carefully for tips on exploring your LAN setup and hints on moving around the LAN quickly. Once you have a feel for the directory structure of your network, sketch a layout of it and keep it on file for easy access. (You may even want to keep it next to you. You should usually make two copies, one for the lab documentation file or binder and one for daily referral and use.) If you manage other users, give them a copy of your layout and highlight the areas with which they work. You will find that paper documentation saves time, even in this so-called paperless society.

OBJECTIVES

After finishing this chapter, you should be able to:

1. List the directories that appear as a result of installing NetWare and become familiar with the contents of each directory.

2. Discuss recommended directory tree setup.

3. Review DOS commands relevant to managing files and directories.

4. Recognize the difference among local, logical, and search drives and know NetWare's limitations.

5. Explain what mapping does and how to set up, view, and use maps to aid in moving from one directory to another.

NETWARE DIRECTORIES

Because file servers allow for the sharing of files, it is crucial that the directories that house the files are managed properly and wisely. In this section, NetWare and other directories and how to map to them are explored.

When NetWare is installed, several directories appear as a result: LOGIN, PUBLIC, SYSTEM, MAIL, DELETED.SAV, DOC, DOCVIEW, MHS, and ETC. These directories provide the foundation for the directory structure.

LOGIN

The LOGIN directory contains the files SLIST.EXE and LOGIN.EXE. When logging into a LAN, every user must first go through the LOGIN directory. For example, at the F:\> prompt, enter "LOGIN USER01." Here, LOGIN is a command instructing the computer to run a program called LOGIN.EXE, and USER01 acts as a parameter needed by the program to verify that a particular user is authorized to use the system. The LOGIN.EXE program also checks the security data found in the Novell Directory Services (NDS) to make sure that the user is allowed to log in and meets any requirements to do so. SLIST.EXE is used to find a list of file servers available. SLIST stands for "server list."

If viruses were to infect the system, they would most likely invade this directory first. See Chapter 9 for more details.

PUBLIC

The PUBLIC directory is used often. It contains NetWare user commands and utilities. Everyone with a LAN account normally has access to this directory, unless for some reason the LAN administrator has taken the rights away.

SYSTEM

The SYSTEM directory houses supervisory commands and utilities. Users normally do not have access to this directory.

MAIL

The MAIL directory, made up of user identification directories (ID), holds the login scripts. See Chapter 10 for more details.

```
F:\PUBLIC>dir *.exe/w

Volume in drive F is SYS
Directory of F:\PUBLIC

BREQUEST.EXE    BREQUTIL.EXE    BROLLFWD.EXE    CX.EXE          LOGIN.EXE
NDBCNVT.EXE     NLIST.EXE       NPATH.EXE       RCONSOLE.EXE    TYPEMSG.EXE
ATOTAL.EXE      AUDITCON.EXE    CAPTURE.EXE     COLORPAL.EXE    FILER.EXE
FLAG.EXE        LOGOUT.EXE      MAP.EXE         MENUCNVT.EXE    MENUEXE.EXE
MENUMAKE.EXE    MENURSET.EXE    NCOPY.EXE       NCUPDATE.EXE    NDIR.EXE
NETADMIN.EXE    NETUSER.EXE     NPRINT.EXE      NPRINTER.EXE    NVER.EXE
PARTMGR.EXE     PCONSOLE.EXE    PRINTCON.EXE    PRINTDEF.EXE    PSC.EXE
PURGE.EXE       RENDIR.EXE      RIGHTS.EXE      SEND.EXE        SETPASS.EXE
SETTTS.EXE      SYSTIME.EXE     UIMPORT.EXE     WHOAMI.EXE      WSUPDATE.EXE
WSUPGRD.EXE     NWADMIN.EXE     WBROLL.EXE      WNDBCNVT.EXE

        49 file(s)    13,268,003 bytes
                      64,831,488 bytes free
```

FIGURE 3.1
PUBLIC directory .EXE files.

DELETED.SAV

The DELETED.SAV directory contains files that were previously deleted and have been salvaged. The directory in which they were originally stored no longer exists.

DOC

The DOC directory contains Novell manuals in electronic form.

DOCVIEW

The DOCVIEW directory contains the program that allows the user to view the electronic manuals. The program is called Dynatext.

MHS

MHS stands for "message handling service." The MHS directory is used for electronic mail (e-mail). Besides holding messages sent between users, it also contains special files for handling the messages.

THE PUBLIC DIRECTORY: USER ACCESS

As mentioned, PUBLIC is commonly used on the network, and everyone with an account has access to it. In Figure 3.1, the executable files (.EXE) located in the PUBLIC directory are listed for reference. These executable files are commonly

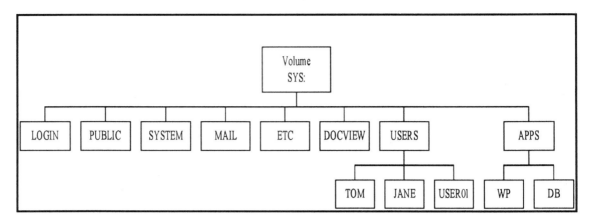

FIGURE 3.2
Sample directory tree structure.

known as utility files, or menu utilities and command line utilities (CLUs). They will be explored in more detail throughout the text.

DIRECTORY STRUCTURE

Users must be granted permission to directories to use, modify, or make files in them. Granting permission is commonly called assigning rights. Rights are discussed later in this chapter.

When assigning rights, do not give users too many rights to the main directories. Avoid assigning rights that give users the power to create, delete, or modify in these directories. In addition to the main directories, some companies add others. Normally, applications branch off from one or two directories, and user home directories branch off a directory called USERS (see Figure 3.2). To create subdirectories, use the DOS make directory (MD) command, Window's file manager, or NetWare's FILER menu utility. (FILER is discussed in Chapter 5.)

With the NetWare LAN system, the directory structure consists of the file server name (optional unless working in a multiserver environment), the volume name, and the directory name, in that order.

NETWORK DRIVE MAPPING

Maps serve to give directions on how to get from one place to another. Similarly, LAN mapping allows the user to move from one directory to another. For example, instead of having to key in a long change directory command such as CD \APPS\WP\ WPERF\GRAPHICS several times during a particular session, the user can set up a map drive to get to this directory more quickly.

Look at the following example:

```
MAP H:=SERV1/ABC_SYS:USERS\TOM
```

Here the file server is called SERV1, the volume (drive) on the file server is called ABC_SYS:, and the directory structure follows USERS\TOM.

As mentioned, maps can also be used to move around in the system rather quickly. Consider, for example, that the following map statement has been entered:

```
MAP G:=ABC_SYS:APPS\WP\WPERF\GRAPHICS
```

On most companies' LANs, either a menu or an F:\> prompt appears when logging in. F: represents the root directory or the server's drive. To change to the graphics directory, simply key in G: and press "enter."

The map stays in effect until the user enters a command to change it or executes the LOGOUT command. Mapped drives, also known as network drives, do not stay permanently. Login scripts often contain map commands; this way, the computer system sets up the map every time the user logs in. MAP commands can also be entered at the prompt. Users often map to their home directories (a private directory that houses a user's data).

Mapping is an action. When the NOS encounters a MAP command, the system maps out, or executes, the instruction to create a drive pointer for a particular directory path. A map is simply a pathway built by the NOS. This pathway leads to a particular directory specified in the MAP statement. This pathway is labeled with a drive name, also called a drive pointer.

In this example,

```
MAP G:=ABC_SYS:APPS\WP\WPERF\GRAPHICS
```

Here, the instruction to NOS is to build a pathway (or point the way) to the GRAPHICS directory, as well as to assign the drive pointer or drive name G: to this pathway. This process is called mapping.

Some words of caution are necessary. If the user changes to the graphics drive mentioned earlier, the G:> prompt now appears on the user's screen. What happens if the user keys in CD.. next? The answer is that G: no longer points to the GRAPHICS directory; it points to the directory immediately above it (WPERF). (The map has been altered by the CD command.)

To view the current map settings, key in "map" and press "enter."

SPECIAL MAPPING OPTIONS

Deleting Map Assignments

Sometimes it is necessary to delete or get rid of mapping assignments. NetWare provides a DEL (delete) option for the MAP command that takes care of this rather simply. For example, to delete the map assignment for G:, simply key in the following:

```
MAP DEL G:
```

(*Note:* It is advisable to type "map" by itself first to verify which drive letter you wish to delete.)

Using the NEXT Option

When creating map assignments, the user normally specifies which drive letter should be assigned. By using the NEXT option, the user is asking the network operating system to see what the next available drive letter is and then make the assignment using that letter. In the following example, notice two things: the letter N does not have a colon after it and there is no equal sign. In this example, a map assignment is made to the next available letter for the directory FUNSTUFF:

```
MAP N ABC_SYS:USERS\FUNSTUFF
```

To find out which drive letter actually gets assigned in this case, the user may key in "map" by itself after the assignment has been made. For further discussion of network drive maps, see Chapter 4.

SEARCH DRIVE MAPS

Users who have worked with DOS may have used the DOS PATH command. When working with the DOS, PATH aids the computer in finding .EXE, .COM, and .BAT files. For example, a user would like to execute a word-processing application file. The file name is WP.EXE, and it is located in the C:\WP directory. If the user's screen has C:\> on it and WP followed by "enter" is keyed in, then the WP.EXE file executes. For a path to work, the user does not have to go to the working directory first. Similarly, on a LAN, if a search map already points to the word-processing directory, then it doesn't matter which prompt appears on the screen. Keying in WP and pressing "enter" executes the WP.EXE file.

An example of a DOS path command is

```
PATH C:\;C:\DOS;C:\WINDOWS;C:\WP
```

An example of a user running the WP.EXE executable file from a C:\> prompt is

```
C:\>WP enter
```

When trying to execute WP.EXE, the computer will first look in the current directory (wherever the user's prompt so indicates). It will next check each directory path listed in the PATH statement until it finds the program file WP.EXE. If it does not find that file, the user will receive the error message "Bad Command or File Name." For further discussion of search drive mapping, see Chapter 4.

Running Application Software Programs

Users share applications that are stored on the file server's hard drive. Search drives are convenient in that they allow users to run applications without having to search through various directories to find them.

An example of a search map pointing to the word-processing directory located under the software applications directory is

```
MAP S3:=ABC_SYS:APPS\WP
```

When at the F:\> prompt, the user keys in WP and presses "enter":

```
F:>WP enter
```

Note: The word-processing program would run even though the user is at the F:\> prompt instead of at the F:\APPS\WP> prompt. The search map told the system where to look for executable files. WP.EXE is an executable file. The extension .EXE does not have to be included when running an executable file; it is assumed by the system.

Running User Commands

A very common application of search drive maps is in reference to user commands. As mentioned earlier, PUBLIC is a general-access directory. It contains user command line utilities (CLUs) and menu utilities. It would be very inconvenient to change the directory (CD) to the PUBLIC directory every time the user wants to execute a CLU or menu utility; thus a search drive map points the way to PUBLIC.

An example of a search map pointing to the PUBLIC directory that houses the user's commands is

```
MAP S1:=ABC_SYS:PUBLIC
```

An example of entering the SEND command line utility to relay a message to another user is

```
F:>SEND "Are you ready for lunch?" TO JANE
```

Note: The user did not have to switch to the PUBLIC directory for the SEND command to work properly. The SEND command resides in the PUBLIC directory; however, the search map assignment to PUBLIC enabled the system to find it with no problems. SEND is only one of many CLUs available in PUBLIC. Other CLUs are discussed in Chapter 6.

S1: is commonly mapped to the SYS:PUBLIC directory, and this particular map command is placed in the system login script by the LAN administrator. Notice that S1 replaces the need for a drive letter. S1: stands for "first search." S1: instructs the computer where to search first if .EXE or .COM files do not reside in the current directory.

When the user assigns a search map S1:, the computer assigns the letter Z: to it. The computer starts with Z: and goes backward through the alphabet as needed until the letter K: is reached. Normally, the maximum number of search drives is 16 (Z: to K:). For each search drive map that the user wishes to use, he or she must first use a MAP command for it. This is unlike the DOS PATH command, where multiple directories may be specified on one line. Usually, up to

21 logical network drives (F: to Z:) and five local drives (A: to E:) are permitted. (See Figure 3.3.) This may change if the local drive uses more than five drives.

Looking for the NEXT Search

With search drive mapping, there is no NEXT option like there is in network drive mapping. This search drive map, for example, instructs the computer where to look to find WP.EXE, a word-processing executable file. When not sure how many search drive maps are in use (S1:, S2:, and so forth), administrators usually specify S16:. For example,

```
MAP S16:=SYS:APPS\WP
```

This approach of mapping to S16: is quite commonly used in login scripts for added flexibility when setting up search drive maps for users and is discussed in Chapter 10.

When the system encounters a search map asking for S16:, it simply finds the next available search. This is because the system does not assign searches out of order. It assigns SEARCH1 first, then SEARCH2, then SEARCH3, and so on.

Search drive maps are often used for pointing to application directories, and regular network drive maps are often used for pointing to data directories. Search drives and network drives are also referred to as *pointers*. If the MAP command is used by itself, it will show which network and search drives are currently mapped in the computer's memory.

SOFTWARE INSTALLATIONS

As long as a user has creation privileges in a given directory, he or she can install software to it, just as on a regular hard drive, with slight changes. For example, if the command for installing a particular software is normally INSTALL C:, on a LAN it may be INSTALL G:; thus, the newly created directory is mapped as drive letter G:. In cases where the user simply wishes to do a straight copy of files from a local drive to a network drive, the DOS COPY command or the NetWare's NCOPY command may be used: COPY A:*.* G: or NCOPY A:*.* G:.

TRUSTEE DIRECTORY RIGHTS

To work with a given directory, the user must first have been entrusted to use that directory by the administrator or the owner of that directory. In other words, the user must have certain *trustee directory rights*. Depending on the user's needs, the administrator may give all or some of the following rights:

R	Read	Allows a user to read the contents of files
FS	File Scan	Allows a user to search through file names (DIR)
W	Write	Allows a user to write to or make changes to a file

Network drives from F:-Z:	Search drives from Z:-K:
F:	Z:
G:	Y:
H:	X:
I:	W:
J:	V:
K:	U:
L:	T:
M:	S:
N:	R:
O:	Q:
P:	P:
Q:	O:
R:	N:
S:	M:
T:	L:
U:	K:
V:	
W:	**Local drives from A:-E:**
X:	A:
Y:	B:
Z:	C:
	D:
	E:

FIGURE 3.3

Logical network drives versus search drives.

C	Create	Allows a user to create a new subdirectory or file
E	Erase	Allows a user to delete a subdirectory or file
M	Modify	Allows a user to change file attributes and file names
AC	Access Control	Allows a user to entrust others to a directory
S	Supervisor	Allows a user all rights to the directory

SUMMARY

Search drives help users run programs without having to change directories. Logical network drives aid in the process of moving from one drive to the next. Local drives at the workstation normally consist of the letters A: to E:. Trustee directory assignments specify the rights that a user has to use particular directories.

EXERCISES

1. Define the following:
   (a) logging in
   (b) salvaged files
   (c) Dynatext
   (d) utility files
   (e) network drive map
   (f) search drive map
2. What do these acronyms stand for?
   (a) MHS
   (b) SLIST
   (c) e-mail
   (d) CLU
3. Compare the differences and similarities of local, logical network, and search network drives.
4. List the main directories of NetWare. What purpose does each directory serve?
5. How would you create the following directories?
   (a) ABC_SYS:-----/USERS---/USER01
   (b) USER02
   (c) USER03
6. How would you map to USER01 through USER03 directories?
7. How would you make a search map to DB? (See Figure 3.2.)
8. Are maps permanent? If not, what suggestions can you make to overcome this limitation?

9. Why is it important to assign directory rights to users?

10. Is it important to document the assigning of directory rights? If so, why? How would it be done?

LAB 3

This lab presents a hands-on application of directory management. In this lab, you will create a directory tree, organize files in the tree, and gain experience working with creating, revising, and printing maps.

1. Make the following directory tree structure *under your home directory.*

QTR1			QTR2			QTR3			QTR4		
JAN	FEB	MAR	APR	MAY	JUN	JUL	AUG	SEP	OCT	NOV	DEC

2. Check to see which drive letters are available:

```
F:\>MAP
```

If a printer is available, print your map for handy reference:

```
F:\>MAP > PRN
```

3. Next, assign map drive letters for each month in your tree structure. Be careful not to key in a letter already in use. For example,

```
F:\>MAP I:=ABC_SYS:USERS\USER01\QTR1\JAN
```

(See your instructor or LAN administrator for help in choosing your directory path.)

4. Double check your map when you are done:

```
F:\>MAP>PRN
```

5. Test your map by changing to each directory. Simply type in the letter you assigned, type a colon, and press "enter." Do this for each directory:

```
F:\>I:
```

You should see the prompt on your screen change to indicate that your computer is now pointing to a different directory. For example,

```
I:\USERS\USER01\QTR1\JAN>
```

6. Friends of yours will be visiting you in January. Make a note of it in the appropriate directory. Make sure to print the note. *Hint:* Switch to January's directory, then create a DOS text file using the editor. For example,

```
F:\>I:"enter"
I:\USERS\USER01\TR1\JAN>EDIT VISIT.TXT
```

See Chapter 2 for a review of the DOS editor.

7. You just found out that there will be a sale on lawn furniture in May. Make a note of it under May. Make sure to print the note when done. There are a few ways to print your file:

   a. While in the DOS editor, choose "print" from the file menu.

   b. From the prompt, use the DOS TYPE command:

   ```
   I:\USERS\USER01\QTR1\JAN>TYPE VISIT.TXT>PRN
   ```

   c. From the prompt, use NetWare's NPRINT command:

   ```
   I:\USERS\USER01\QTR1\JAN>NPRINT VISIT.TXT Q=PRINTQ_1
   ```

   PRINTQ_1 is an example of a print queue name. A print queue is a waiting line for jobs that need to be printed. See your LAN administrator or an instructor for the names of available print queues.

8. December is your vacation. Make and print a note.

CHAPTER FOUR

NETUSER UTILITY

INSPIRING MOMENT

Congratulations on your new promotion; you have worked hard for it. In addition to having a new office, you also have a new account on the network. You want to get off to a good start by staying organized. You want to have both the directories for the users for whom you are responsible and your directories well organized in a tree fashion. You also want to communicate and work well with people in a professional manner. How do you accomplish all this?

Some people have briefcases, containers, boxes, and so forth, to organize tools used most often; such organization leads to a day that flows smoothly. Tools are easy to find. Similarly, organized files with labels on them make it easy to access important papers as they are needed. In Chapter 3, you explored directory management and learned how files are grouped into different directories according to their function. You also learned that map drives make finding and working with the files in these directories more manageable. In this chapter, you will build on the foundation set forth in Chapter 3. You will learn where to go to create map drives and will explore other options available, such as selecting your printer and sending messages. The goal is to stay organized, and NET-USER makes it easy to do so.

QUESTIONS FOR THOUGHT

Is your daily life organized? Do you have to search everywhere to find a pencil, a pen, paper, or maybe a computer disk? Do you constantly dig through an unorganized file cabinet that contains files with no labels? Could an LAN environment help you? What are some benefits of having an organized LAN environment? Would it be beneficial to have an easy way to find files and directories on the LAN? Would the users at the organization for which you work (or plan to work for) benefit from being able to send messages?

CHALLENGE

In Chapter 3, directory structures and mapping were explored. Use the skills that you have acquired, plus NETUSER, to organize your home directory. Also, set up your system so that you can go to your subdirectories and run software ap-

FIGURE 4.1
NETUSER's available options menu.

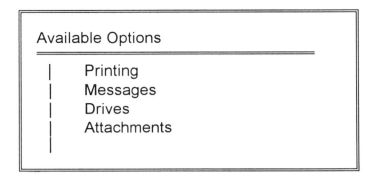

plications quickly. As you learn how to send messages with the NETUSER utility, respect people's rights and feelings. A LAN should be free of obscenity or profanity. See the common courtesy rules found in the Preface. Keep your working environment clean and professional, and have fun!

OBJECTIVES

After finishing this chapter, you should be able to:

1. Move between file servers if working in a multiserver environment.

2. Create logical drive mappings with NETUSER.

3. Create search drive mappings with NETUSER.

4. View a list of users and groups currently logged in.

5. Send messages to users and groups.

6. Change the default drive.

NETUSER OPTIONS

In the NetWare networking environment, tools used daily are found in a PUBLIC menu utility called NETUSER, which allows a user to access data files quickly, run software application programs, find out who is currently logged in and send messages to those people, and switch between different file servers.

NETUSER provides a menu orientation to several commands normally encountered during a particular work session. Common NETUSER commands include MAP, USERLIST, and SEND. (See also command line utilities in Chapter 6.) The "Available Topics" menu (Figure 4.1) appears when NETUSER is keyed in.

PRINTING

Printing and sharing of printers is a major reason companies choose to have a LAN system. After all, not many companies can afford to attach a laser printer to each user's computer, and even if they could afford it, it would not be financially responsible. Users do not normally spend 100 percent of their time printing; more often, they spend time planning, developing, and creating on the computer. Printers are used to print the output or results once everything else is done. It is no wonder that companies choose to have users share printer hardware resoruces via a LAN.

Network Printers

Network printers are actually defined and set up using other utilities such as PCON-SOLE. (See Chapter 7 for more information on PCONSOLE.) The NETUSER menu utility allows users to share printers once the setup is complete. By selecting "printing" from NETUSER's available options screen, a list of the workstation printer ports (available ports) will appear on the screen.

Printer Port

A printer port may be set up as either a local or a network printer port. A local printer port is used when a private printer is attached to a specific workstation solely for one user's individual use. With network port assignments, the local operating system (DOS) is tricked into thinking that the printer is attached to the workstation; actually, the printer may be across the room, far away from the actual workstation making the printing request. From the available ports screen, users can control whether the printer ports are designated as local or network ports.

Assigning a Port for Network Use

The following steps are used to designate that the port is to point to a network printer:

1. To assign the port as a network port, first highlight the port of interest and press "enter."
2. Next, select "change printers."
3. A list of printers and print queues (waiting line for print jobs) appears. Highlight either a printer or a print queue and press "enter." If no printers or print queues appear on the list, then press "insert" and choose a different context in which to search for the printer or queue.

Recall from Chapter 1's discussion of context that the NDS is organized in an upside-down treelike design. This upside-down tree is broken up into organization containers ("O="), organizational unit containers ("OU="), and leaves. A print queue, like a user account, is represented as a leaf inside a container. For example, the accounting department may have a container assigned with the user accounts and print queues represented as leaves within that department's container. Print queues are usually placed in an organizational unit. If the goal is to have just the accounting department able to use a particular printer's queue (or waiting line), the printer's queue is placed in that department's container.

FIGURE 4.2
NETUSER's available options
submenu for messages.

```
┌─────────────────────────────────────────┐
│ ╔═══════════════════════════════════════╗│
│ ║  Available Options                     ║│
│ ║ ═══════════════════════════════════════║│
│ ║  | Send Messages to Users              ║│
│ ║  | Send Messages to Groups             ║│
│ ║  | Set Receive Message: OFF            ║│
│ ║  |                                     ║│
│ ║                                        ║│
│ ╚═══════════════════════════════════════╝│
└─────────────────────────────────────────┘
```

Check Jobs Waiting to Print

To check the status of a job waiting to print, such as a report, memo, or program source code, follow these steps:

1. Choose "printing" from the NETUSER menu.
2. Choose the port to which the job was sent.
3. Select "print jobs." A list of print jobs for the chosen port (queues) appears.

MESSAGES

Communication is a prime reason companies opt to use a LAN. Messages may be sent to any user individually or to a group of users, if they are logged in at the time. If they are not logged in, they do not receive the message and the message is not saved for them. Once the "messages" option has been selected from the NETUSER's available options menu, a submenu appears. This submenu contains three choices, shown in Figure 4.2.

Send Messages to Groups

The "send messages to groups" option allows the user to view a list of the names of groups in which at least one member is logged in. It allows a user to send a message to the entire group. This menu is fairly straightforward and easy to use.

Send Messages to User

The "send messages to user" option provides a list of current users logged into the system. It allows a user to view more information regarding another user. It also allows a user to send messages. This option is also straightforward and easy to use.

Set Receive Message

The "set receive message" option allows a user to inform the network operating system whether or not messages are to be received and displayed on that user's screen. If "receive message" is set to OFF, the user is specifying that messages are to be blocked from appearing on the screen. Any users attempting to send a message to that particular station while the receive message setting is off would receive an error message informing the sender that the message was not permitted to go through.

Note that the user and group lists are context sensitive. The users to whom someone is trying to send a message may be in a different department; thus their account name may be represented as a leaf inside a different organizational unit container. Unless the organizational unit in which to find them is specified, they will not receive the messages sent. The context, as discussed in Chapter 1, tells the NOS which organizational unit container to search to find the user. To specify a different context than the one currently set as default, press the "insert" key. Once "insert" has been pressed, NOS will prompt to key in the context for the user to whom a message is trying to be sent. If a context is not specified, the NOS will simply search the current context in the NetWare directory services (NDS). This would result in the NOS not finding users located in other organizational units.

DRIVES

Users frequently find themselves working with drive letter assignments. There are two main types of drives: logical drives and search drives. In both cases, a user takes the file server's hard drive and/or storage media and logically (rather than physically) divides it into smaller sections. The drive is thus more manageable. This section explores logical drives and search drives in more detail.

Drive Mappings

The "drive mappings" option displays current map assignments. If additional map assignments are needed, a user may press "insert" to add them.

As mentioned earlier, one type of network drive assignment is called a "logical" drive assignment. For example, although the file server's volume is labeled "ABC_SYS," the NOS can be instructed to view certain assigned areas of that volume as if the area were a drive by itself. Here the NOS is instructed to view a user's home directory as if it were an H: drive:

```
MAP H:=ABC_SYS:USERS\NUSER01
```

Because there is really no physical drive H:, this drive is commonly referred to as a logical (or pretend) drive.

The Purpose of Logical Drives

Assigning drive letters to long path names allows users to follow a particular path more rapidly. Consider the following examples, and see how fast a user can move to a particular directory once a drive letter has been assigned. In addition, there is less chance of keyboarding errors when drive letters are assigned.

To change to a different directory, the user may key in the change directory (CD) command:

```
F:\>CD \USERS\NUSER01
F:\USERS\NUSER01>
```

To change to a different directory that already has a logical drive letter assigned, the user may simply key in the drive name, such as H:, and press "enter." On the screen, it looks like this:

```
F:\>H:
H:\USERS\NUSER01>
```

Notice that this last example has 15 fewer keystrokes to enter than the first example!

Although the time savings shown above was only 15 keystrokes, consider the savings during an eight-hour day in which a user constantly moves between different directories.

Logical drive mappings also cut down the number of keystrokes needed for entering many of the DOS commands and NetWare command line utilities (CLUs). Instead of long path names, users can key in the logical drive name. Consider the following example of NetWare's NCOPY command line utility:

```
NCOPY H:\*.* A:
NCOPY ABC_SYS:USERS\NUSER01\*.* A:
```

Both examples accomplish the same task. All the files in the NUSER01 directory are copied to the floppy disk in drive A:. The first example, however, requires fewer keystrokes because H: is already mapped to the path ABC_SYS:USERS\NUSER01. NCOPY and other CLUs are discussed in Chapter 6. Commonly used DOS commands are discussed in Chapter 2.

It is advisable to put the map assignment commands used most often in a login script. Map drive assignments are not permanent; they reside in the workstation's RAM. When a user logs out, these assignments are no longer in effect. If the MAP command is placed in a login script, then every time the user logs in, the map assignment is re-created in RAM.

NETUSER and Drive Mapping

NETUSER can be used to view current map assignments and to add new ones. Keep in mind that once a user logs out, any maps not found in the login script will no longer be in effect. If a user wishes to have the new map assignment for every logging in session, the following way of creating a map assignment is *not* recommended. On the other hand, if a user is working on a special project and only needs the map assignment for this particular project, then using NETUSER in this way is recommended.

To process a map assignment using the temporary approach, follow these steps:

1. Key in the word "netuser" to access the menu utility.
2. From the available options menu, select "Drives."

3. From the drives menu, select "Drive Mapping." A list of current drive mappings will now appear.
4. Press the "insert" key to indicate to the network operating system to add a new drive assignment.
5. When the prompt asks you if you want to map the new drive assignment as a directory root, answer no. If you answer yes, your prompt will appear as H:\>, for example, instead of H:\USERS\NUSER01>. Most users prefer to have the screen prompt display the path in which they are working.
6. When prompted, fill in the directory path.

Logical Drives

Assigning logical drive names allows users to move quickly to different directories. Logical drive names allow users to enter DOS commands and CLUs with fewer keystrokes than otherwise, thus saving valuable time. Logical drive assignments commonly point to directories containing the user's personal data, such as in these examples:

```
MAP H:=ABC_SYS:USERS\NUSER01
MAP I:=ABC_SYS:USERS\NUSER01\PROJECTS
MAP J:=ABC_SYS:USERS\NUSER01\LETTERS
```

A user can easily work with personal data files found in these subdirectories. By the way, the highest directory level for a particular user is called the user's home directory, which in this example is ABC_SYS:USERS\NUSER01. Logical drives, as mentioned, are assigned by using the MAP command line utility or the NETUSER menu utility. Logical drives usually point to the user's home directory and other subdirectories containing data files. A directory that contains files used by more than one user is called a shared data directory. Logical drives may also point to shared data directories, as illustrated here:

```
MAP K:=ABC_SYS:USERS\REDTEAM
MAP L:=ABC_SYS:SHARED\CLIENTS
```

Logical drive assignments greatly ease the task of managing home directories and other subdirectories assigned to individual users. They also make it easier to manage shared data directories. Logical drive maps normally point to data directories. Search drive maps normally point to application directories. The next section discusses search drive maps and the DOS PATH command, which make it easier and faster to access program or executable files located in application directories.

DOS PATH Command

Because the NetWare search map is similar to the DOS PATH command, reviewing the DOS command will help when learning the LAN counterpart.

The PATH command is often located in a file called AUTOEXEC.BAT. To check, use this command:

```
C:\>EDIT AUTOEXEC.BAT
```

Remember that AUTOEXEC.BAT is like cruise control on a car. This batch file automatically runs every time the computer is cold booted (turned on) or warm booted (reset). Any commands placed in the file will execute at the time of booting. Consider the following PATH statement:

```
PATH C:\;C:\WINDOWS;C:\DOS;C:\WP;C:\DB
```

This command provides the local operating system—in this case, DOS—a list of directory paths through which to search if a program was requested and that program was not immediately found. For example, with

```
C:\>WP
```

the user is attempting to run the word-processing program called WP.EXE. Note that in DOS, if an executable file ends with .EXE, .COM, or .BAT, it is not necessary to key in the file's extension. This command would not immediately result in the execution of the WP.EXE program. The local operating system, DOS, would first need to locate the WP.EXE file before it could run it. In the above example, the computer would do the following:

1. It would look through the root directory of the C: drive for the WP.EXE program, with no success.
2. Next, it would look through the C:\WINDOWS directory with no success.
3. It would then look through the C:\DOS directory, with no success.
4a. Finally, it would look through the C:\WP directory, find the WP.EXE program, and run it.

    or

4b. If, after searching all the directories listed in the PATH statement, the program was not found, an error message, "Bad Command or File Name," will appear.

PATH versus Search Mapping

The NetWare search map works in the same way as the DOS PATH statement, with two major exceptions. First, a separate map assignment, or command, is needed for each directory path through which the user wishes the network operating system to search. Second, it's common to use search map assignments to define directory paths for running programs or applications that are stored on the file server's volume. Consider the following example:

```
MAP S1:=ABC_SYS:PUBLIC
```

Here the search map assignment conveys to the network operating system that the PUBLIC directory, located on volume ABC_SYS:, is the first place it should look for an executable file if it's not found in the current directory.

The WHOAMI command is actually a program (WHOAMI.EXE) located in the PUBLIC directory. It provides information about who is logged in at the workstation where the command was keyed in.

```
F:\>WHOAMI
```

Note that if the message "Bad Command or File Name" comes up at this point, the user should check to ensure that a search map has been assigned to the PUBLIC directory. Once again, because maps are temporary, any MAP command that a user anticipates using each time he or she logs in should be placed in a login script. NETUSER may be used to make both temporary logical drive map assignments and search map assignments.

To assign a search map using NETUSER, follow these steps:

1. Key in the word "*netuser.*"
2. Select "Drives" from the available topics menu.
3. Select "Search Mapping" from the drives menu. A list of currently assigned search maps appears.
4. Press "insert" to indicate to the network operating system that a search map drive is about to be created.
5. When prompted to do so, key in the directory path for the search.

ATTACHMENT

Before a user can log in to the network, the workstations must first be "attached" to a file server. *Attached* means that the file server acknowledges that the computer is not just a stand-alone PC; it's a workstation capable of operating in the LAN environment. Recall from Chapter 1, that key files have to be installed on the PC before it's truly a workstation. The workstation installation process resulted in the creation of a directory called C:\NWCLIENT. The C:\NWCLIENT directory contains open datalink interface (ODI) files needed to announce to the network's file server that the PC is a workstation. Once the ODI files have been executed, the workstation is attached to, or recognized by, a file server on the network.

It is possible to have more than one file server on the same network. In a multiserver environment, a user may attach and log in to more than one file server during a single work session. The attachments option found in the NETUSER menu utility allows a user to hop over to another file server, so to speak; once recognized by or attached to the other file server, the user is prompted for an account name and password. The "attachment" option is located on NETUSER's main menu.

Once attachment is selected, another menu appears. This new menu allows users to select which file server to which they wish to attach by selecting the "server information" option from the attachment menu. When selected, server information lists servers to which the user is currently attached and logged in. A user may switch between these servers by simply highlighting the one interested in and pressing "enter." A user is already logged in to the servers appearing on this list; therefore, pressing "delete" on any of them results in the user being logged out of that particular file server. The "insert" key brings up another list of servers, those to which the user has not yet logged in but which are available for use. Highlighting a server sends a signal to the new file server that the workstation would like to be recognized and log in. The new server then prompts the user for an account name and password. The attachment submenu also gives the option of changing your login script and password. The steps are straightforward once the attachment submenu is reached. Follow the directions found on the screen.

Attachment is fairly versatile; it allows a user to hop between file servers already logged in to; it allows a user to attach and log in to file servers that the user is not yet recognized by, and it also allows the user to change his or her login script and password. Login scripts are discussed more in Chapter 10.

SUMMARY

The NETUSER utility is fairly straightforward. It provides an easy way to create logical and search drive maps, to change between servers, to send messages, and to change a user's login script and password.

EXERCISES

1. Define and/or explain the following:
   (a) attachment
   (b) port
   (c) network printer
   (d) logical drive
   (e) search mapping
   (f) "Bad Command or File Name"
2. Where is the NETUSER utility located, and who can use it?
3. The "attachments" option is frequently used in what environment?
4. How do you send messages to a user using NETUSER? How else can you send messages?
5. How do you send messages to a group using NETUSER? How else can you send messages?
6. How do you create logical drive maps using NETUSER? How else can you create them?
7. How do you create search drive maps using NETUSER? How else can you create them?
8. How can you change the default drive using NETUSER? How else can you change it?

LAB 4

This lab will give you a chance to practice routine tasks that most users encounter daily. By the end of this lab, you should be able to create both logical and search drive maps assignments. You should also be able to send messages to individual users and to a group of users. You will have the opportunity to put the map assignment into your user login script so that it will automatically execute every time you log in. You will also practice changing your password. You will be managing your LAN environment today using NETUSER. By the end of the lab, you should discover that NETUSER is powerful yet fairly easy to work with.

1. Make a subdirectory inside your home directory. Next, map to that directory.
2. Map a search drive to one of the application directories to which you have rights.
3. Send a message to everyone in your group.
4. Send a message to a friend.
5. Add the maps assignments to your login script. (Test the login script.)
6. Change your password.
7. List the name(s) of the file server(s) available to you.

CHAPTER FIVE

FILER UTILITY

INSPIRING MOMENT

Congratulations, you are performing well at your new network administration position. Your supervisor and colleagues continually compliment you on your expertise in NetWare 4.1. Friday marks the end of your 90-day probationary period, and you can hardly wait! This company prides itself in choosing only the very best people to hire permanently. Once you become a permanent staff member, you are then entitled to company benefits such as paid vacations, medical insurance, and a 401K retirement plan. You notice that your supervisor has already begun to complete the temp-to-perm review forms required for all new personnel. As she fills out the review forms, your supervisor watches you more closely than ever before. You know that you have done well up to this point, yet you are nervous. The pressure of the final week as a temporary worker reminds you of preparing for finals at school.

As the week progresses, you continue to do your best. The Marketing Research Department has called on you to organize several of their statistical files on the computer. You recall lessons on directory management and carefully plan which files are going to be copied to which directories. The marketing team has been working all year on these statistical research files, so there are quite a few of them. They have data files from various surveys conducted by the survey teams throughout the community. They also have some custom-built programming applications designed especially for the marketing department for the analysis of the survey data. You are happy that you remember the steps for creating directories and assigning maps to the directories. Everything is going well. Then it happened!

You accidentally copied the statistical marketing programs on top of the survey data files. You accidentally chose "OK" when it asked to "overwrite existing file." The program files had the same name as the data files, so the data files accidentally got overwritten. Now what? The marketing team has invested a lot of time in these files! You inform your supervisor immediately. She walks out of her office without a word and leaves the building. You can tell that she is upset.

QUESTIONS FOR THOUGHT

Could this happen to you? What would you do if it does? Are there some precautions that you can take to prevent something like this from happening? Is there some way to get the lost files back? How do you think this would affect a new employee's review? Do you think that the way that the situation is handled will make a difference in how the supervisor reviews a new employee?

CHALLENGE

Find out as much as you can about managing files and directories. Practice file management operations as much as you can. When you are the person responsible for managing files, have an organized system for backing up your work. Also, acquaint yourself with the salvage options that allow you to bring back files that have been accidentally deleted. In any case, do your best. We all learn from our mistakes. This chapter explores FILER, a menu utility that helps managing files. Read on to learn how you can manage files effectively.

OBJECTIVES

After finishing this chapter, you should be able to:

1. Find the FILER utility and execute it.
2. Identify the options available through the FILER utility.
3. Explore information available on directories.
4. Explore changing drive pointer defaults.
5. View file information under a given directory.
6. Manipulate subdirectories by copying and moving files.
7. List the various FILER options that can be set by the user.
8. View information regarding the file server's volume.
9. Salvage files that have been accidentally deleted.
10. Purge (or permanently delete) files to make more space on the file server's hard drive.

FILER

FILER, which is shorthand for "file maintenance," allows for the management of directories and files. Users can explore different settings and can, if authorized, make changes in settings. Many of the tasks available under FILER can also be accomplished through command line utilities. In addition, the FILER utility of NetWare has a salvage feature that allows files to be brought back if they are accidentally deleted. NetWare also has directory and file attributes that can be placed on the files and directories to prevent accidental erasing.

FIGURE 5.1
FILER's available options menu.

```
Available Options
════════════════════════════════════════
|Manage Files and Directories
|Manage According to Search Patterns
|Select Current Directory
|View Volume Information
|Salvage Deleted Files
|Purge Deleted Files
|Set Default Filer Options
|
```

NetWare's PUBLIC directory houses user menu utilities and command line utilities. The FILER menu utility, located in this PUBLIC directory, has options that appear similar to familiar DOS commands. See Figure 5.1. Although many of these topics are explored in detail in the end-of-chapter lab, brief descriptions are given here.

SELECT CURRENT DIRECTORY

To check information regarding a different directory, the "select current directory" option should be chosen. If users do not remember the name of the directory, then after they choose "select current directory," they may press the insert key and the system will provide a list of directories from which to choose. After keying in or selecting the directory of interest, the user may choose the selection "manage files and directories" again.

MANAGE FILES AND DIRECTORIES

When a user selects "manage files and directories," the directory contents submenu appears on the screen (see Figure 5.2). This screen lists the files and directories contained under the directory currently chosen. At this point, the user has several options:

1. Change the directory path to a different level.
2. Manage one or more subdirectories.
3. Manage one or more files.
4. View and/or set directory information.

Change the Directory Path to a Different Level

There are three basic ways to move in the NDS tree:

1. To move back one level in the directory tree, a user should highlight ". . (parent)" and press "enter."

FIGURE 5.2
FILER's directory contents
screen.

Directory Contents	
• •	(parent)
\	(root)
•	(current)
ETC	(subdirectory)
LOGIN	(subdirectory)
MIGRATE	(subdirectory)
PUBLIC	(subdirectory)
SYSTEM	(subdirectory)
TTS$LOG.ERR	(file)
VOL$LOG.ERR	(file)

2. To move all the way back to the root directory, a user should highlight "\ (root)" and press "enter."

3. To move forward in the directory structure, a user should highlight one of the subdirectories, such as the PUBLIC directory in Figure 5.2. Once the subdirectory is highlighted, press "enter."

Once the subdirectory has been selected, the next step is to manage either the subdirectory or the files contained in the subdirectory.

Manage One or More Subdirectories

To manage a particular subdirectory, a user should highlight the subdirectory of interest from the directory contents menu (see Figure 5.2). Once the subdirectory has been highlighted, press the "select" key, which is the F10 function key. After pressing F10, the "subdirectory options" submenu appears, as shown in Figure 5.3. From this menu a user can then copy, move, check rights, or view the directory information for the subdirectory selected.

To work with more than one subdirectory at a time, highlight each subdirectory, one by one, from the directory contents menu and press the "mark" key, which is the F5 function key. After marking each of the subdirectories of interest, press the F10 select key. A submenu called multiple subdirectory options appears on the screen; see Figure 5.4. This submenu offers fewer options than the subdirectory options menu. The user may copy the subdirectories and set and/or view the owner's name, creation date, and rights. Note that to set—that is, to change—any information, the user must have the rights to do so.

```
┌─────────────────────────────────────────────────┐
│ ┌─────────────────────────────────────────────┐ │
│ │                                             │ │
│ │   Subdirectory Options                      │ │
│ │  ═══════════════════════════════════════    │ │
│ │                                             │ │
│ │  │Copy Subdirectory's Files                 │ │
│ │  │Copy Subdirectory's Structure             │ │
│ │  │Move Subdirectory's Structure             │ │
│ │  │Make This Your Current Dir                │ │
│ │  │View/Set Directory Information            │ │
│ │  │Rights List                               │ │
│ │                                             │ │
│ └─────────────────────────────────────────────┘ │
└─────────────────────────────────────────────────┘
```

FIGURE 5.3
Subdirectory selected from FILER's directory.

Manage One or More Files

Users may choose to manage files in the same manner as that given for subdirectories. A user should select the files by highlighting the file name and pressing the F10 select key while at the directory contents menu. If there are multiple files, the user highlights them one by one and presses the F5 mark key. Once all the files of interest are selected, the user then presses the F10 select key.

Next, either the file options or the multiple file operations submenu will appear on the screen. See Figures 5.5 and 5.6. The file options menu allows a user to copy, move, view, check rights, and view and/or set the file's information details for a given file. The multiple file operations screen does not permit the moving of the files, but users may choose to copy them.

```
┌─────────────────────────────────────────────────┐
│ ┌─────────────────────────────────────────────┐ │
│ │                                             │ │
│ │   Multiple Subdirectory Operations          │ │
│ │  ═══════════════════════════════════════    │ │
│ │                                             │ │
│ │  │Copy subdirectories' files                │ │
│ │  │Copy subdirectories' structure            │ │
│ │  │Set owner                                 │ │
│ │  │Set creation date                         │ │
│ │  │Set inherited rights                      │ │
│ │                                             │ │
│ └─────────────────────────────────────────────┘ │
└─────────────────────────────────────────────────┘
```

FIGURE 5.4
Multiple subdirectory operations selected from FILER's directory contents.

```
File Options
─────────────────

 | Copy File
 | Move File
 | View File
 | Rights List
 | View/Set File Information
```

View and/or Set Directory Information

Who owns a particular subdirectory? When was it created? Are there any special attributes (such as hide files) applied to this subdirectory? What rights does a particular user have to a particular directory? Which users have been entrusted to use a particular subdirectory? If one is allowed to save files to this subdirectory, is there a space limit? If so, how much?

These questions are all addressed by the directory information screen. There are two ways to get to the directory information screen:

1. From the directory contents submenu, select the directory of interest by highlighting the subdirectory's name and pressing "enter." Next, highlight "• |(current)" (see Figure 5.2) and press "enter." "View/set directory information" should appear. Press "Enter" again to select this option.
2. Another way to get to the directory information screen is to select "view/set directory information" from the subdirectory options menu.

```
Multiple file operations
─────────────────────────

 | Copy marked files
 | Set owner
 | Set creation date
 | Set last modified date
 | Set last accessed date
 | Set attributes
 | Set inherited rights
```

FIGURE 5.6
Multiple file operations selected from FILER's directory contents.

The directory information screen contains the following details regarding the particular subdirectory selected:

- Directory owner
- Date created
- Time created
- Directory attributes
- Inherited rights
- Trustees
- Limit space (yes/no)
- Directory space limit: nnnn kilobytes

Assign Trustees and Their Rights Using the Directory Information Screen

Recall from the discussion in Chapter 3 regarding directories that to use a particular directory, users must have permission. Those who have been granted permission to use a particular directory are called *trustees* of that directory; they have been entrusted to use the directory properly. The extent to which they can use the directory is governed by the assignment of rights. Rights dictate to the system what the users can or cannot do inside the directory for which they have been assigned as a trustee. The rights available in NetWare 4.1 include the following:

- File scan: The trustee may view a listing of file and subdirectory names within the assigned directory.
- Read: The trustee may view the contents of the files located in the assigned directory.
- Create: The trustee may create files and subdirectories within the assigned directory.
- Write: The trustee may overwrite and make changes to files and subdirectories within the assigned directory.
- Erase: The trustee may remove files and directories within the assigned directory.
- Modify: The trustee may change the attributes (such as hidden) for files and subdirectories contained in the assigned directory.
- Access control: The trustee may assign other users as trustees for this particular directory and any files or subdirectories contained inside it. The trustees may only assign up to the level of rights that they have been assigned.
- Supervisory: The trustee has all the rights mentioned to the assigned directory and for all subdirectories contained therein. Note that all the other rights can be blocked or prevented from applying to lower-level directories; once the supervisory right has been assigned, it applies to the NDS tree structure from the point assigned going down into the directory levels below and cannot be blocked.

From the directory information screen, new trustees may be assigned for the current directory. To assign a new trustee for the currently selected directory, highlight "trustees" and press "enter." A list of current trustees for this directory appears on the screen. Press the insert key and the system will prompt for the account name of the new trustee. If a user changes his or her mind, a trustee can be removed from the list by highlighting the trustee's account name and pressing the delete key. Once the trustee's account name has been added to the trustee list, the default rights of read and file scan are assigned. To change this assignment—that is, to add more rights or lessen the number of rights assigned—do the following:

- Once again, go to the trustees list for that directory. Do this by highlighting and pressing "enter" where it says "trustee" on the directory information screen.
- Highlight the particular trustee of interest and press "enter."
- A list of assigned rights will appear on the screen. To remove one of the rights from the list, simply highlight the right that is to be removed and press the delete key. To remove more than one right, use the F5 (mark) key to mark each of the unwanted rights, and then press "delete."
- To add more rights, press the insert key. A list of rights not yet assigned for this user will appear on the screen. Highlight the right needing to be added and press "enter." To add more that one right, use the F5 mark key to select them, then press "insert." Press "escape" when done to return to the directory information screen.

The directory information screen provides a short summary of security and management aspects regarding the directory. It also allows a user to modify the assignment of trustees and their rights to particular directories. Be aware, however, that to make such modifications, the user must have the access control right, which gives permission to give that person's rights away to other users.

MANAGE ACCORDING TO SEARCH PATTERNS

Search patterns are helpful if a user wants to view just a particular set of file or subdirectory names. For example, a user may want to see all the file names that have an extension of .BAT if the file names start with the word PROJECT but not with the word PROJECT1. Setting up a search pattern can accomplish this. When the user selects "manage according to search patterns" from FILER's main menu, the screen called "set the search pattern and filter" appears on the screen, as displayed in Figure 5.7.

Exclude Directory Pattern

The "exclude directory pattern" option tells the computer which subdirectories a particular user does not want to see in the directory listing. This does not delete subdirectories; it just does not show their names in the directory list.

Include Directory Pattern

The "include directory pattern" option lets a user specify if only certain subdirectories should show in the directory listing.

Exclude and Include File Patterns

The "exclude and include file patterns" option is similar to the exclude and include options for directories. It allows a user to specify which files to show in a directory list.

```
┌─────────────────────────────────────────────────────────────────────┐
│                  Set the search pattern and filter                    │
├─────────────────────────────────────────────────────────────────────┤
│                                                                       │
│   Pattern:   *.*                                                      │
│                                                                       │
│   Exclude directory patterns:  ↓ (empty)                              │
│   Include directory patterns:  ↓ *                                    │
│                                                                       │
│   Exclude file patterns:  ↓ (empty)                                   │
│   Include file patterns:   *                                          │
│                                                                       │
│   File search attributes:   ↓ (empty)                                 │
│   Directory search attributes:  ↓ (empty)                             │
│                                                                       │
└─────────────────────────────────────────────────────────────────────┘
```

FIGURE 5.7
FILER search pattern and filter screen.

File Search Attributes

The "file search attributes" option allows a user to specify if he or she wants to see files in which the attribute flag has been changed. (An attribute is the state or characteristic of the file. One such attribute is "hidden"; see the Chapter 6 discussion on the command line utilities FLAG command for other examples.)

Directory Search Attributes

The "directory search attributes" option is the same as file search attributes except that it deals with subdirectories instead of files. See the Chapter 6 discussion on the FLAG command for a list of directory attributes.

VIEW VOLUME INFORMATION

When chosen from FILER's Available Topics menu (see Figure 5.1), the "view volume information" option provides basic information regarding the file server's volume (hard drive).

WORK WITH DELETED FILES

It's wise to plan for the unexpected, especially when working with networks. Novell did just that by adding the salvage and purge options to their FILER menu utility. The salvage option lets a user rescue deleted files. The purge option lets a user permanently get rid of them.

Salvage Deleted Files

The "salvage deleted files" (see Figure 5.1) option allows a user to retrieve files that have been previously deleted as long as the files have not been purged (*purged* in this sense means "instructed to never come back"). If the directory in which the files were originally located still exists, the files will be returned to that directory. If not, they will be restored to a directory named DELETED.SAV. The DELETED.SAV directory resides right off the SYS volume (ABC_SYS:DELETED.SAV). DELETED.SAV will not appear in the directory list because it has the directory attributes hidden and system assigned to it.

To salvage a file from the currently chosen directory, choose "salvage deleted files" from FILER's main menu. Three options appear: "view/recover deleted files," "salvage from deleted directories," and "set salvage operations." By selecting "view/recover deleted files," a list of salvageable files will appear. Highlight the file of interest and press "enter." If there is more than one file to bring back, the F5 (mark) key may be used to select them. Answer yes to confirm the operation. Files salvaged using this option are restored to the directories from which they were deleted.

If the directory from which the file was deleted no longer exists, choose "salvage from deleted directories" and proceed as directed above. Files salvaged using this option are restored to the DELETED.SAV directory.

Notice that by selecting "set salvage options," a user may request to see the file names in a particular order. The possibilities are by file name, file size, deletion date, or deletor.

Purge Deleted Files

Sometimes, because of a need for more storage space or for tighter security, it is necessary to delete one or more files permanently. To purge files, select "purge deleted files" from FILER's main menu. Upon doing so, two options appear. "Purge current directory files only" indicates that a user only wishes to delete files in the current chosen directory, whereas "purge the entire subdirectory structure" includes not only the currently chosen directory but also any subdirectories found inside (or under) that directory.

When prompted for the file pattern, a user may type in a particular file name. Note that the asterisk (*) indicates that the user wants to purge all files.

SET DEFAULT FILER OPTIONS

Set Default Options

From FILER's main available options menu, the "set default filer options" option is available, as shown in Figure 5.1. This option allows a user to structure the computer's response to certain commands or operations.

When the "set default filter" option is selected from FILER's main menu,

```
┌─────────────────────────────────────────────────────────────────┐
│                         FILER Settings                          │
├─────────────────────────────────────────────────────────────────┤
│                                                                 │
│  Confirm deletions:  No                                         │
│                                                                 │
│  Confirm file copies:  No                                       │
│  Confirm file overwrites:  Yes                                  │
│                                                                 │
│  Preserve file attributes:  Yes                                 │
│  Notify if name space information is lost:  No                  │
│                                                                 │
│  Copy files sparse: No                                          │
│  Copy files compressed: No                                      │
│  Force files to be copied compressed:  No                       │
│                                                                 │
└─────────────────────────────────────────────────────────────────┘
```

FIGURE 5.8
FILER settings.

the filer settings screen appears, as shown in Figure 5.8. If a user presses the delete key while highlighting a directory or file name, should the system prompt with a confirmation message, such as, "Are you sure?" or should it simply delete the file? The following section discusses various options for which a user can customize the computer's response.

Confirm Deletions

If set to yes, the "confirm deletions" option instructs the computer to double check with the user after a deletion command has been entered and before actually deleting a file. If set to no, then when a delete instruction is given, the system will delete files without asking the user, "Are you sure?"

Confirm File Copies

The "confirm file copies" option, which is similar to the "confirm deletions" option, will give an "Are you sure?" or similar prompt when a copy command has been entered.

Confirm File Overwrites

If a user attempts to copy a file to another file name and the file name to which the user is copying, the destination file, is already in use, the system will interpret this to mean that the file being copied is supposed to replace this destination file.

This replacement process is called overwriting. The "confirm file overwrites" option asks the computer to double check with the user if the destination file name of a write instruction would result in overwriting a file.

SUMMARY

FILER provides an easy way to check and change file and directory settings as well as a way to see directory listings in a particular manner. Subdirectories can be organized in a way that makes it easy to find needed files. Moving, copying, deleting, salvaging, or purging of files can be accomplished with ease. Once users have mastered working with FILER, they can perform the daily management of files and subdirectories successfully.

EXERCISES

1. Define the following:
   (a) confirm (deletions, file copies, and so forth)
   (b) include directory pattern
   (c) file search attribute
   (d) salvage deleted files
   (e) purge deleted files
2. What does FILER stand for, and where is it located? What does it allow you to manage?
3. How does FILER let you look at a different directory than the one you are using?
4. What information about directories can be found through FILER?
5. What information about files can be found through FILER?
6. What information about the file server's volume can be found through FILER?
7. How do you copy a file using FILER?
8. How do you copy all files in a particular subdirectory using FILER?
9. What does FILER stand for?
10. Who or what is a trustee?
11. What rights must you have to assign a trustee?
12. What file attributes are available in NetWare?
13. What FILER option allows you to see hidden files?
14. How do you delete a file using FILER?
15. How can you determine the owner of a particular file through FILER?
16. Why is the salvage option used?
17. Why is the purge option used?

LAB 6

In this lab, you will get first-hand experience with working with the FILER menu utility. This lab takes you on a short tour of FILER and lets you take an inside look at your home directory. You will also have the opportunity to give some of your rights to another user. By the end of this lab, you should have a greater appreciation for the power and simplicity of FILER.

Getting Started and Selecting Your Directory

1. Key in the word *FILER* and press "enter" to get started.

```
F:\>FILER
```

2. In the space provided, write down the available options for FILER.

Available Options

3. Choose "select current directory" from FILER's main menu, and key in the directory path for your personal directory when prompted to do so. Press "enter" when you are done. If you do not know your directory path, see your LAN administrator for assistance. Pressing "insert" may be helpful if you are stuck; it provides a step-by-step walkthrough approach to arrive at your directory. Here is an example of a current directory path:

```
ABC_SYS:USERS\USERXX
```

Here, ABC_SYS: is the name of the volume on the file server's hard drive where the home directory is located. USERS is the name of the subdirectory that houses the user home directories. USERXX is one particular user's home directory.

4. Notice that the "current path" found at the top left corner of your screen has changed. Write down your current directory path before proceeding.

Managing Your Directory

1. Now that your home directory has been selected as the current directory, let's take a look at it. Select "manage files and directories" from FILER's main menu. The directory contents screen now appears. Write down some of the key files and subdirectory names that you notice before proceeding. (If no key files appear, your subdirectory is empty. Perhaps this is a new home directory, and you have not yet saved any work into it. If this is the case, write the word *empty* in the chart below.)

Directory Contents	
• •	(parent)
\	(root)
•	(current)

2. Next, you will work with the directory information screen. Highlight "• |(current)" and press "enter" twice. Fill in the following chart. It will serve as a nice reference document for your home directory.

Information for directory USERXX

Owner:

Creation date:
Creation time:

Directory attributes:
Current effective rights:

Inherited rights filters: [   ]
Trustees:

Limit space:
Directory space limit: Kilobytes

3. What rights do you have to this directory? Look next to where it says "current effective rights." Do you see the first letter of each assigned right listed here? Look up these letters in this chapter's text if you have forgotten what they mean. List your rights below. Write out the word, not just the first letter.

Rights

Assigning Trustees and Rights

Would you like to give another user permission to use your home directory? Sometimes this is necessary, especially if you are working on a project with someone. (Before proceeding with this lab, you may want to check with the LAN administrator to make sure that this is OK.)

1. From the directory information screen, select "trustees" and press "enter." Next press "insert," select another user's account name from the list that now appears on the screen, and press "enter." If the user for whom you are looking is not on the list, try highlighting "• |(parent)" because that user may be in a different context. "• |(parent)" takes you back a level in the tree; pressing "enter" on a container name moves you forward.

2. Next, you will give your new trustee additional rights. Highlight your new trustee from the trustee list now displayed on your screen. Press "enter." A list of assigned rights now appears. (Notice that by default "read" and "file scan" have been assigned.) Press the insert key to add more rights. Give the user create rights by highlighting "create directory/file" and pressing "enter." Press "escape" when done.

3. Next, you will revoke (deny the use of) the read right for this trustee. Highlight your new trustee and press "enter." Once again, the list of assigned rights now appears on the screen. Highlight "read from file" and press the delete key. Answer "yes" when the "revoke right" prompt comes up. Press "escape" when done. The trustee can no longer read the content of files in your home directory.

4. Finally, you have decided not to entrust this user with your home directory, so you will need to remove that person from the trustee list. Simply highlight the trustee's name and press "delete." Answer "yes" when prompted if you want to delete the trustee. Don't worry: you are not deleting the user's account; you are just taking away the permission to use your directory.

Working with Files

Next, you will explore managing files using the FILER utility.

1. Choose "manage files and directories" from FILER's main menu. You should see a list of files and directories that are located in your home directory. Choose one of your files and press the F10 select key.
2. The file options menu now appears on your screen. Choose "view/set file information." One of the items listed on the file information screen is attributes. You are going to hide the file you have selected by putting an attribute of "hidden" on it. Highlight the word *attribute* and press "enter." A list of assigned attributes appears. (The list is most likely empty at this point.) Press "insert" to bring up a list of attributes not yet assigned. Make a list of the file attributes. This will serve as a good reference tool.

File Attributes

Highlight "hidden" and press "enter." Your file is now hidden.

3. Verify that the file is indeed hidden. To do so, choose "managing files and directories" again from FILER's main menu. Notice that when the directory contents screen appears this time, your file no longer exists. You successfully hid the file.

Managing According to Search Pattern

Sometimes it is necessary to look for particular file names. In this case, you would like to view files that are currently hidden. Normally, the directory contents screen does not display hidden files, but you can instruct the system to search for them.

1. Choose "manage according to search pattern" from FILER's main menu. Select

"file search attributes" and press "enter." You will see a list of already assigned attribute searches now appears on the screen; it is most likely empty. Press the insert key to add a new attribute to the attribute search screen. A list of attributes not yet chosen appears on the screen. Highlight "hidden" and press "enter." You have now added the hidden attribute to the file search attributes. To see the results of this request, press the F10 (continue) key. A listing for the currently chosen directory appears. Even though your file is flagged as being hidden, it now appears on the screen in the directory list. Press Alt F10 (quick exit) to get out of FILER quickly.

2. Be aware that even though you just saw your file, it is still hidden. To prove this point, exit FILER all the way by pressing Alt F10 (fast exit). Use the DOS DIR command to view the directory listing. You should be at your home directory for this step:

```
F:\USERS\USERXX>DIR/W
```

Notice that the file you hid does not appear in the directory listing.

3. Since you may need to work on this file at a later date, you need to practice unhiding files. Go back to FILER to unhide your file:

```
F:\USERS\USERXX>FILER
```

Select "managing files and directories" from FILER's main menu. Once again, notice that your hidden file is not listed. When you left FILER and went to the DOS prompt, the system reset the search pattern back to normal.

4. Press the "escape" key to return to FILER's main menu. You need to set the file search pattern again. Choose "manage according to search pattern." Next, select "file search attributes." Now press "insert" and choose "hidden." Press the F10 (continue) key. Notice that you have successfully requested the system to search your directory and to include files that have the hidden attribute in the resulting directory listing.

5. Next, you want to unhide your file. To do so, first, highlight your file and press the F10 (select) key. You should now see the file options submenu on your screen. Details regarding attributes are located on the file information screen. Select "view/set file information" at this time. Highlight "attributes" and press "enter." This file's current attributes are now displayed on the screen. Highlight the "hidden files" attribute and press "delete." Confirm the deletion by choosing "yes." You have now completed the steps for unhiding your file.

6. To verify that the file is indeed unhidden, first, exit FILER by pressing Alt F10 (quick exit). You should be at your home directory for this next step. Display a directory listing for your home directory.

```
F:\USERS\USERXX>DIR/W
```

Notice that your file now appears in the directory listing. You were successful in unhiding your file. You should practice hiding and unhiding files until you feel competent doing so. Repeat steps 1 through 6 here until you are comfortable with the process.

Copying Files Using FILER

Copying files is a very common task that users perform routinely. In this portion of the lab, you will practice the copy procedure.

1. Make sure that you have already selected your home directory, and go back into FILER.

    ```
    F:\USERS\USERXX>FILER
    ```

2. Choose "managing files and directories" from FILER's main menu. Next, highlight the file you would like to copy. We will call this particular file the source file. In computer terms, *source* consists of the directory path of the file copying from. Press F10 (select) to proceed. The file options menu now appears on your screen. Select "copy file" and press "enter."
3. The system now prompts you for your destination directory. *Destination* means where you are going to put the newly copied file. In this case, make sure your home directory is entered as the destination: ABC_SYS:USERS\USERXX, for example. Press "enter" after putting in your destination directory's name.
4. The computer will now prompt you for the destination file name. Enter the name that you wish to call the new file. For this example, call your file NEW-FILE.TXT. If you were copying to a different directory and you wanted to keep the same name, you could have simply pressed "enter." But because you are copying to the same directory, you cannot use the same file name, so you must provide a different file name.
5. Press "escape" to return to the directory content's screen. You should now see the new file in the directory listing. You have successfully completed the procedure for copying the file. Review and practice steps 1 through 5, copying files, until you feel competent.

Deleting Files Using FILER

It is advisable to go through your directories periodically and delete any files no longer needed. By doing so, you will free up disk space and make your directories and files more manageable.

1. Once again, go into FILER (if you are not already there). Select your home directory (if it's not already chosen). Select "managing files and directories" from FILER's main menu.
2. Highlight the file you wish to remove. For this example, highlight NEW-FILE.TXT, which was created as the result of the file copying procedure. Once the file name is highlighted, press the DEL "delete" key. Confirm the deletion by choosing "yes." You have now successfully deleted the file.

Viewing Volume Information

It is particularly helpful to know where your files are being saved. "Volume information" gives details about the file server's volume. Remember that a volume is located on the file server's hard drive or on a disk subsystem that is attached to the file server. A disk subsystem is a unit that contains multiple storage devices such as hard drives. A disk subsystem can also contain a CD-ROM drive.

1. You would like to get information about the volume that contains your home directory. Go into FILER and select "view volume information" from FILER's main menu.
2. Fill in the details that you discover about the volume.

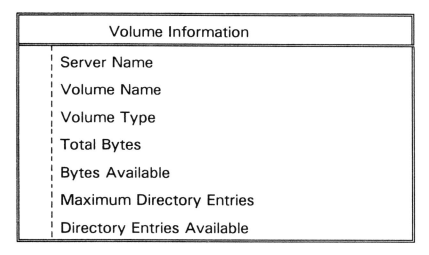

Volume Information
Server Name
Volume Name
Volume Type
Total Bytes
Bytes Available
Maximum Directory Entries
Directory Entries Available

Lab Summary

You have now successfully completed the FILER lab. FILER is fairly easy to use; it's powerful, and it can do quite a few things. Go through the steps found in this lab several times until you are familiar with them.

COMMON TASKS

Part III explores everyday operations such as printing and command line utilities.

CHAPTER SIX

COMMAND LINE UTILITIES

INSPIRING MOMENT

You are working at your new position in the Data Processing Department. Networking is new to you, and you hear other people in the department discussing commands for the network. When you get stuck with a problem, they often ask you if you have tried a particular command. You don't want to sound like a novice, yet there are so many commands that you have been running into daily that you wonder if you will ever learn them all. You may even think to yourself, "I wonder how long I can survive in this company before they find out that I don't know what I'm doing." You feel that all the prior training you have had with computers is useless and was perhaps a waste of time. That prior experience listed on your resume doesn't seem to make you an asset to this company. Your confidence level may not be very high at the moment.

QUESTIONS FOR THOUGHT

Could exploring and practicing the most commonly used command line utilities (CLUs) help you perform better? Could you benefit by having a reference list of commonly used CLUs to refer to as needed? Could you benefit by sharing notes and questions with your colleagues who are also trying to improve their ability in using CLUs? Could you benefit by saying the commands and how they are used into a tape recorder, and then playing back the tape during the day? Could you benefit by implementing another system of learning that you know of or have used in the past? Do you think it would be beneficial to review the CLUs periodically, even before you have to really use them in a work environment? Would this periodic review of CLUs improve your retention and help you feel more confident in using them? Do you think that negative self-talk is beneficial for improving your performance in a LAN environment? Do you think most LAN administrators know everything there is to know about networking? What kinds of self-talk are beneficial for improving your performance?

CHALLENGE

Do not be afraid to experiment with a new way of learning something. Decide which system of learning works best for you, and write it down in your own words. Keep your written notes in a file, and make a copy of them so that they are available to you. Share with others. If you are able to explain something to someone else, not only do you help others, but you reinforce your own understanding and knowledge of that subject. Don't be hard on yourself. If CLUs seem a little overwhelming at first, give yourself time and keep practicing. Start with the commonly used CLUs, and add to your learning every day. Many CLUs work similarly to local operating system commands (such as DOS), so do not tell yourself that the time you spent learning the local operating system and other commands was useless. You will be an even greater asset to your current or future organization if you are comfortable working in both the local operating system and network operating system environments.

OBJECTIVES

After finishing this chapter, you should be able to:

1. Identify the location of command line utilities.
2. Explain the importance of mapping to the PUBLIC directory.
3. Explore the most commonly used command line utilities.
4. Distinguish the command line utilities from menu utilities.

COMMAND LINE UTILITIES BASIC COMMANDS

As the name implies, command line utilities (CLUs) are entered on the command line, which is commonly referred to as the prompt. If a user has worked in the DOS environment, he or she will find many similarities between NetWare commands and DOS commands.

CLUs are located in the PUBLIC directory and have an .EXE extension. Users have access to these commands. CLUs differ from menu utilities in that the instructions are not in a menu format; instead, the instructions are simply keyed in. There are many CLUs, but in this chapter, the discussion is limited to those commands used most often.

Caution: Because these commands are located in the PUBLIC directory, users must always have a search map drive pointing to the PUBLIC directory. Most organizations will have this set up in the system login script.

ROUTINE SYSTEM COMMAND LINE UTILITIES

Routine system CLUs include logging in and out of the network, finding the file server's current time, changing the user's password, and finding what version of NOS is loaded on the file server.

LOGIN

LOGIN allows a user to sign on to the LAN.

LOGIN /NS

LOGIN /NS allows a user access to the network without executing the login scripts. This is particularly useful if the login script contains an error that is causing problems while logging in. It's also useful if the login script is lengthy and the user just needs to log in briefly to do a simple task, such as send a message to another user.

LOGIN SERV2/USERXX

LOGIN SERV2/USERXX allows a user to log in to a different file server than the one set as default. A user may be logged in to more than one file server simultaneously. Simply put the file server's name, followed by a slash (/), and then key in the user's account name for that particular file server.

LOGOUT

LOGOUT allows a user to sign off the LAN.

LOGOUT SERV2

LOGOUT SERV2 allows a user to log out of a particular file server (in this case, SERV2). If no file server name is specified, the user is logged out of the entire network.

SYSTIME SERV2

The SYSTIME command allows a user to see the date and time on a particular file server to which he or she is attached. This function is particularly useful if the server is out of the state or the country and is handy in a wide area network (WAN) environment.

To view the time on the current server, use the same command without specifying the file server name:

```
F:\PUBLIC>systime
Current system time: Thursday 5-18-95 2:03:58 pm
```

SETPASS

The SETPASS command allows a user to change his or her password.

SETPASS SERV2/

SETPASS SERV2/ allows a user to change the current password assigned for a particular file server (in this case, SERV2).

```
F:\PUBLIC > npath
Based on the following workstation information:
    Current working directory: F: = CN = ABC_SYS: \PUBLIC
    Utility load directory: F: = CN = ABC_SYS: \PUBLIC
    NWLANGUAGE = ENGLISH
    PATH = Y:.;C:\NWCLIENT\;C:\WINDOWS;C:\;C:\DOS;C:\WPWIN;C:\DB;C:\WP

The search sequence for message and help files is:
    F: = CN = ABC_SYS: \PUBLIC
    F: = CN = ABC_SYS: \PUBLIC\NLS\ENGLISH
    F: = CN = ABC_SYS: \PUBLIC
    Y: = CN = ABC_SYS: \PUBLIC
    C:\NWCLIENT
    C:\WINDOWS
    C:\
    C:\DOS
    C:\WPWIN
    C:\DB
    C:\WP
    F: = CN = ABC_SYS: \PUBLIC\NLS\ENGLISH
```

FIGURE 6.1
NPATH command.

NVER

The NVER command displays the version of NetWare currently in use.

NPATH

The NPATH command allows a user to view the path currently assigned in memory (see Figure 6.1).

COMMUNICATING ON THE NETWORK

As discussed in Chapter 1, a key benefit of having a network is the ability to communicate with others. The following CLUs help users find out who is currently logged in to the network, to specify if messages should be received or blocked, and then to send messages to other users or groups of users.

NLIST	General Help Screen	4.19

NLIST	General Help Screen	4.19
Purpose: View information about users, groups and other objects. Syntax: NLIST class type [property search option] [display option] [basic option]		
For details on:	Type:	
Property search options	NLIST /? R	
Properties	NLIST /? P	
Display options	NLIST /? D	
Basic options	NLIST /? B	
All Help Screens	NLIST /? ALL	
Class types:		
* (all class types)	User	Print Queue
Server	Group	Printer
Computer	Volume	Print Server
Directory Map	Profile	Organization
Organizational Unit	Alias	AFP Server
Enclose in double quotes all class types or properties containing spaces.		

FIGURE 6.2
NLIST command.

NLIST USER/A

The NLIST command displays a list of all the users currently logged in (see Figure 6.2). Key in NLIST /? for a listing of other available options.

NLIST User SHOW "Telephone," "Street Address"

The command NLIST User SHOW "Telephone," "Street Address" displays a list of telephone numbers and addresses for the users.

WHOAMI

WHOAMI displays what name under which a user is logged in. Various options can be applied to this command. To see a listing of the options, add /? to the end of the command.

WHOAMI/ALL

The WHOAMI/ALL command displays information about the user currently logged on to the station (see Figure 6.3). The /ALL option gives all the details. By adding the /ALL option, the system will display security information regarding the user

```
F:\PUBLIC>whoami

Current tree:  ABC_CO
Other names: Nancy Blackmon Velasco
Title:         LAN Instructor
Description:   for CBS/Operations Courses


User ID:      Nancy.CONSULTANTS.abc_co
Server:       ABC  NetWare 4.10
Connection: 3 (Directory Services)
```

FIGURE 6.3
WHOAMI command.

and list the groups of which this user is a member. A shorter version of the WHOAMI command that does not give all the details is also available.

SEND "How about lunch? TO USER11; SEND "Can someone help me?" TO LANCLASS

The SEND commands allow a user to send messages to another user or to an entire group.

SEND/A=C

The SEND/A=C command allows a user to block messages from being received by his or her station. All messages except console messages are blocked. Console messages are sent by the console operator who monitors activity on the network.

SEND/A=N

The SEND/A=N command allows a user to block all messages from being received by his or her station. All messages, including console messages, are blocked.

SEND/A

The SEND/A command removes the message blocks placed by SEND/A.

MANAGING DIRECTORIES WITH COMMAND LINE UTILITIES

CLUs for managing directories allow users to assign drive maps, rename directories, manage directory rights, copy an entire directory, and manage directory attributes.

```
F:\PUBLIC > map

Drives A,B,C,D,E map to a local disk.
Drive F: = ABC_SYS: \PUBLIC
Drive H: = ABC_SYS: \USERS\NANCY
Drive Z: = ABC_SYS: \PUBLIC
      -----   Search Drives   -----
S1: = Y:. [ABC_SYS: \PUBLIC]
S2: = C:\NWCLIENT\
S3: = C:\WINDOWS
S4: = C:\
S5: = C:\DOS
S6: = C:\WPWIN
S7: = C:\DB
S8: = C:\WP
```

FIGURE 6.4
MAP command.

MAP G:=SYS:USERS\USER05; MAP S4:=SYS:APPS\WP

The MAP commands allow a user to create a logical or search drive mapping to point to a particular directory. See Figures 6.4 and 6.5. Chapter 3 provides more details on the MAP command.

MAP INS S4:=SYS:APPS\WP

The INS S4 option instructs the system to create a new search drive map and make it the fourth directory path searched. If another directory path is already set as the fourth search path, the one that is already set will move down and become the fifth search path.

MAP DEL G:

MAP DEL G: instructs the system to remove the drive mapping for drive letter G:.

MAP N SERV2/SYS:APPS\PROJECTS

The N (next) option instructs the system to create a new logical drive map and assign it the next available drive letter.

MAP	General Help	4.12

Purpose: To assign a drive to a directory path.
Syntax: MAP [option | /VER] [search: = [drive: =]] | [drive: =] [path] [/W]

To:	Use:
Insert a search drive.	INS
Delete a drive mapping.	DEL
Map the next available drive.	N
Make the drive a root directory.	R
Map a drive to a physical volume on a server.	P
Change a regular drive to a search drive or a search drive to a regular drive.	C
Display version information	/VER
Do not change master environment.	/W

For example, to:	Type:
Map the next available drive to the login directory on server FS1	MAP N FS1/SYS:LOGIN
Map drive W: as a search drive to the WP directory	MAP S16: = W: = APPS:WP

FIGURE 6.5
MAP command help.

MAP S16:=SYS:APPS\DB

The S16: option instructs the system to assign the next available search sequence to the given directory path. Remember that the system does not assign search numbers out of order. Thus, even though S16 may be requested, if S4: was the last number assigned, S5 would automatically be used next.

RENDIR USER\USER05\PRACTICE USER\USER05\KEEPIT

The RENDIR command allows a user to rename a directory.

RIGHTS SYS:USERS\USER05

The RIGHTS command displays a user's rights to a particular directory (see Figure 6.6). If the directory path is not specified, the default directory will be used.

```
F:\PUBLIC > rights
ABC\SYS:\PUBLIC
Your rights for this directory: [SRWCEMFA]
    Supervisor rights to directory.          (S)
    Read from a file in a directory.         (R)
    Write to a file in a directory.          (W)
    Create subdirectories and files.         (C)
    Erase directory and files.               (E)
    Modify directory and files.              (M)
    Scan for files and directories.          (F)
    Change access control.                   (A)
```

FIGURE 6.6
RIGHTS command.

RIGHTS SYS:APPS\WP /T

The /T option instructs the system to display a list of trustees who have been assigned rights to a particular directory. If the directory already has a drive letter mapped to it, the shortcut for this command can be used:

```
RIGHTS G: /T
```

In this example, the trustees for the directory path to which the drive letter G: points would be displayed on the screen.

RIGHTS SYS:APPS\WP /I

The /I option instructs the computer to display a list of users who have inherited rights to this directory. When a trustee is assigned rights to a particular directory, the user being assigned the rights automatically inherits the same rights for any subdirectories contained within the directory to which the rights were originally assigned. Therefore, the user has what is called *inherited rights* to the subdirectories. The inherited rights are assigned automatically, unless the person who has supervisory rights to the subdirectory has placed an inherited rights filter on the subdirectory. An inherited rights filter (IRF) specifies which rights are allowed to trickle down. If there is an IRF on the subdirectory, any rights not listed in the IRF, even though they may have been initially assigned as trustee rights in the upper directory, do not go into effect. Even though the user initially inherited rights to the subdirectory, the rights may have been filtered out. Effective rights refer to the actual rights to a given directory that apply once the IRF has been taken into consideration. Trustee rights are not filtered out by IRF at the level they were assigned, because trustee rights are direct assignments at that particular directory level. Consider the following example.

In the directory SYS:APPS\WP, user INSTRUCTA has been assigned RFCEW rights. This is a direct assignment. If any IRFs are assigned to this same directory level, it would not affect INSTRUCTA's assignment. INSTRUCTA's trustee rights are RFCEW and they are not blockable; therefore, INSTRUCT's effective rights (usable ones) are the same (RFCEW).

In the directory SYS:APPS\WP\TUTORS, user INSTRUCTA does not have any assigned rights, but because SYS:APPS\WP is at the directory level above this one, INSTRUCTA inherits the rights (RFCEW) that trickle down from where they were assigned. There is no IRF set on this particular directory; therefore, INSTRUCTA's inherited rights are not filtered out, and RFCEW become the effective rights at this level.

In the directory SYS:APPS\WP\TUTORS\SPECIAL, user INSTRUCTA does not have any assigned rights, but because SYS:APPS\WP is at a directory level above this one, RFCEW rights trickled down. Since there were no IRFs at the directory level right above the current level, INSTRUCTA inherited rights become RFCEW rights. Suppose, however, that the user who has supervisory rights to this directory now decides to place a filter on the directory SYS:APPS\WP\TUTORS\ SPECIAL. Suppose that the IRF is set to RFM. Even though user INSTRUCTA has inherited rights of RFCEW, they have been filtered out to allow only the ones listed in the IRF to become effective. In this particular case, R and F are the only two that become effective rights. Notice that even though M is shown in the IRF example, it does not go into effect because it does not have an initial trustee assignment of M (modify).

RIGHTS SYS:APPS\WP\TUTORS\SPECIAL RFCEW
/NAME=INSTRUCTA,USERXX

The /NAME option allows a user to assign trustee rights to other users or groups. Notice that the list of rights to be assigned goes immediately prior to /NAME, followed by the users' account names. Note that if a drive map has already been assigned to the particular path, the RIGHTS command can be shortened as follows:

```
RIGHTS G: RFCEW /NAME=INSTRUCTA,USERXX
```

FLAG H:*.* RO /S /DO

The FLAG command with the /DO option allows a user to set directory attributes. In the command, *.* means that all the files in this directory are to be flagged. The attribute RO stands for "read-only." The /S option instructs the system to flag files located in subdirectories. In NetWare, the directory attributes include the following:

N   Normal

H   Hidden

P	Purge
Dc	Don't compress
Dm	Don't migrate
Sy	System
Di	Delete-inhibit
Ri	Rename inhibit
Ic	Immediate compress

MANAGING FILES WITH COMMAND LINE UTILITIES

NDIR

The NDIR command allows a user to view the names of files in a particular directory. It is similar to the DOS DIR command but more detailed.

NMENU MYMENU

The NMENU command allows a user to run a particular menu that has already been created.

NCOPY G:MYTEST.TXT A:MYTEST.BAK

NCOPY is the NetWare copy command for copying files. See Figures 6.7 through 6.9. NCOPY is very similar to the DOS COPY command. Wild cards can be used with this command. A number of special options can be applied to NCOPY. For a listing of them, key in NCOPY /?.

NCOPY H:*.* I:*.* /S

One popular option is to include subdirectories, and the /S option allows users to accomplish this. With this command, all files and subdirectories located in the directory path assigned to drive H: are copied into the directory path assigned to drive I:. (Recall from the DOS review in Chapter 2 that *.* means all files.)

PURGE H:*.*

The PURGE command instructs the computer to remove any deleted files permanently. Recall from the Chapter 5 discussion of FILER that if a file is deleted, it can be salvaged as long as it has not been purged. Purging files clears out any files that have been deleted from the disk. Once they have been purged, they can no longer be salvaged. It's a good idea to execute the PURGE command once a month to free up space on the hard drive. Depending on the amount the LAN is used at a facility, this command may be executed more or less often than once a month. Purging is also useful for maintaining security of highly sensitive files. Once the files are no longer needed, it is a good idea to delete and then purge them. In

NCOPY	General Help	4.13
Purpose: To copy files and directories.		
Syntax: NCOPY source path [target path] [options]		

To:	Use:
Copy subdirectories	/S
Copy subdirectories including empty directories	/S/E
Copy files with archive bit set	/A
Copy files with archive bit set, then clear the bit	/M
Copy sparse files	/F
Inform when non-DOS file information will be lost	/I
Copy only DOS information	/C
Read after write verify on local drives (DOS only)	/V
Retain compression on supported media	/R
Retain compression on unsupported media	/R/U
Display version information	/VER

For example:	Type:
To copy all files and subdirectories from volume SYS to drive G:	NCOPY SYS:*.* G:*.* /S

FIGURE 6.7
Examples of NCOPY.

```
Example without map short cuts:

H:\USERS\NANCY>ncopy h:\users\nancy\one\hi.txt h:\users\nancy\two\hi.txt

  From H:\USERS\NANCY\ONE\
  To   H:\USERS\NANCY\TWO\
  HI.TXT      (13)

  1 file was copied.
```

FIGURE 6.8
NCOPY help.

```
Example with map shortcuts:

H:\USERS\NANCY > map i: = sys:users\nancy\one

Drive I: = ABC_SYS: \USERS\NANCY\ONE

H:\USERS\NANCY > map j: = sys:users\nancy\two

Drive J: = ABC_SYS: \USERS\NANCY\TWO

H:\USERS\NANCY > ncopy i:hi.txt j:hi.txt

  From I:\USERS\NANCY\ONE\
  To   J:\USERS\NANCY\TWO\
  HI.TXT        (13)

  1 file was copied.
```

FIGURE 6.9
MAP and NCOPY examples.

the command PURGE H:*.*, all deleted files found in drive H: directory are permanently removed.

PURGE H:*.* /S

The /S option of the PURGE command instructs the system to purge deleted files from subdirectories contained inside the directory to which the drive letter H: is pointing.

FLAG SYS:USERS\USER01\MYTEST.TXT RO /FO

The FLAG command allows a user to change file attributes. When no attributes are specified, the current attribute settings for that particular file are displayed. Wild cards are allowed. Recall from the DOS review in Chapter 2 that * is a wild card, which stands for all files. Consider the following:

```
FLAG G:*.* RO /FO
```

The following is an example of using the flag command:

H:\USERS\NANCY > flag

Files   = The name of the files found
Directories   = The name of the directories found
DOS Attr   = The DOS attributes for the specified file
NetWare Attr   = The NetWare attributes for the specified file or directory
Status   = The current status of migration and compression for a file
                  or directory
Owner   = The current owner of the file or directory
Mode   = The search mode set for the current file

Files	DOS Attr	NetWare Attr	Status	Owner	Mode
41SCREEN	[Rw---A]	[-----------------]		.Nancy.CONS...	N/A
41MAP	[Rw---A]	[-----------------]		.Nancy.CONS...	N/A
41SCRNS.95A	[Rw---A]	[-----------------]		.Nancy.CONS...	N/A
PUBDIR41.595	[Rw---A]	[-----------------]		.Nancy.CONS...	N/A
SCRN41B.595	[Rw---A]	[-----------------]		.Nancy.CONS...	N/A
SCRN41C.595	[Rw---A]	[-----------------]		.Nancy.CONS...	N/A
SCRN41D.595	[Rw---A]	[-----------------]		.Nancy.CONS...	N/A
SCRN41E	[Rw---A]	[-----------------]		.Nancy.CONS...	N/A

FIGURE 6.10
FLAG command.

All files in the drive G: directory would be flagged as read-only. See Figure 6.10.
    The /FO option stands for "file attribute." In the above example, RO stands for "read-only." The following attributes can be applied to files.

Ro	Read-only
H	Hidden
P	Purge
Di	Delete-inhibit
Sh	Shareable
Ci	Copy-inhibit
Dm	Don't migrate
Dc	Don't compress

ALL	All
Rw	Read-write
Sy	System
A	Archive-needed
Ri	Rename-inhibit
T	Transactional
X	eXecute-only
Ic	Immediate compress
Ds	Don't suballocate
N	Normal

Commonly used options and their descriptions are as follows.

Ro   Read-only means that the users cannot make changes to the file; they can only read it. Note, however, that if users have been assigned modify rights, the Ro flag can be removed. Recall that the modify right gives users the authorization to change file attributes.

H   Hidden means that the file is really there, but it is hidden so that it does not appear in the regular directory listing. Recall from the FILER discussion in Chapter 5 that the user can still see the hidden files in the directory listing by going to FILER, for example, and viewing them through the search pattern option.

P   Purge means that after this attribute is set on a particular file, if it is ever deleted for whatever reason, it is to purge immediately, with no chance of salvaging it.

Sh   Shareable means that more than one user can access the file at a time. This very common attribute is used for files that are located in application directories where programs are located. It gives permission, for example, for user A to run it at the same time as user B.

Rw   Read-write means that the contents of a file may be viewed and changed. Note that for this attribute to be advantageous, the user must also have RFW trustee rights.

A   Archive-needed is a flag that the system puts on a file when the file is either new or has been modified in some way since the last backup was done.

X   The execute-only attribute does not allow users to view, copy, or change the contents of the file. The user is only allowed to run the file. Once the execute only attribute has been applied, it cannot be removed. If a change is needed, the original software disks have to be reloaded onto the system.

CONTROLLING PRINTING WITH COMMAND LINE UTILITIES

As mentioned in Chapter 1, one benefit of having a LAN is the ability to share hardware resources. To print on a network, several extra steps are needed than when printing on a stand-alone PC. Printing is discussed further in Chapter 7. This section acquaints you with some commonly used CLUs associated with printing.

CAPTURE	General Help	4.10

Purpose: CAPTURE allows you to redirect DOS and OS/2 print
   jobs to a network printer (or file) from an application
   designed to print to a parallel (LPT) port. It also
   allows you to print screen text to a network printer.

Syntax: CAPTURE [options]
Options:
 Create (CR = < path >) - Create a file to store printed data in.
 Server (S = < NetWare bindery server >) - Specify the NetWare
      server containing the bindery queue you
      want to send the print job to.
 Job (J = < configuration >) - Specify the print job
      configuration name to be used.
      You can also specify the context in which to look
      for a configuration if it is outside the current
      search path by identifying the container or user
      owning the configuration:
         J = < configuration > : < context >
 Hold (HOLD) - Send a print job to a queue without having it print.

FIGURE 6.11
CAPTURE options, page 1.

CAPTURE B=SINGERS C=2 FF L=1 Q=PRINTQ_1 S=SERV1 TI=15 NOTI

The CAPTURE command allows a user to specify how future print jobs in this
session will be set up. This is particularly useful when printing from within an
application. The abbreviations used are as follows:

B	Banner name
C	Number of copies
FF	Form feed
L	Printer port number
Q	Name of print queue
S	Name of server

```
┌─────────────────────────────────────────────────────────────────────┐
│ CAPTURE              General Help Page              4.10              │
├─────────────────────────────────────────────────────────────────────┤
│ Job configuration overrides:                                         │
│  LPT port (L = <1-9>)                                                │
│  Keep (K)                                                            │
│  Banner (B = <banner name>)  Name (NAM = <name>)  No Banner NB)     │
│  Form (F = <form or number>)                                        │
│  Queue (Q = <queue name>) Printer (P = <printer name>)              │
│  Copies (C = <1-65000>)                                             │
│  Tabs (T = <1-18>)  No Tabs (NT) (default)                          │
│  Timeout (TI = <0-1000>)                                            │
│  Form Feed (FF)  No Form Feed (NFF)                                 │
│  Autoendcap (AU)  No Autoendcap (NA)                                │
│  Notify (NOTI)  No Notify (NNOTI)                                   │
│                                                                      │
└─────────────────────────────────────────────────────────────────────┘
```

FIGURE 6.12
CAPTURE options, page 2.

TI   The length of time the network should wait once the print command
         has been given to make sure that additional printing is not coming

NOTI   Notify user when the job has printed

Figures 6.11 through 6.13 display the various options that a user can incorporate with the CAPTURE command.

PSC PS=PS0 STAT

The PSC (print server control) command allows users to display the status of the printers and print servers. In the command PSC PS=PS0 STAT, the print server's name is PS0 and STAT stands for "status." Other options available may be discovered by keying in PSC /?.

NPRINT H:MYTEST.TXT Q=PRINTQ_0 B=NANCY FF

NPRINT (see Figure 6.14) is very similar to CAPTURE, with the exceptions that a user also needs to specify the file name being printed and that the settings apply only to this particular print job. (See CAPTURE for comparison.) A description of available options are available by keying in NPRINT /?. Here, the file

```
┌─────────────────────────────────────────────────────────────────┐
│                                                                   │
│  CAPTURE              General Help Page               4.10        │
│                                                                   │
├─────────────────────────────────────────────────────────────────┤
│                                                                   │
│  Job configuration overrides:                                     │
│    LPT port (L = <1-9>)                                           │
│    Keep (K)                                                        │
│    Banner (B = <banner name>)  Name (NAM = <name>)  No Banner (NB)│
│    Form (F = <form or number>)                                    │
│    Queue (Q = <queue name>) Printer (P = <printer name>)          │
│    Copies (C = <1-65000>)                                         │
│    Tabs (T = <1-18>)  No Tabs (NT) (default)                      │
│    Timeout (TI = <0-1000>)                                        │
│    Form Feed (FF)  No Form Feed (NFF)                              │
│    Autoendcap (AU)  No Autoendcap (NA)                             │
│    Notify (NOTI)  No Notify (NNOTI)                                │
│                                                                   │
│                                                                   │
└─────────────────────────────────────────────────────────────────┘
```

FIGURE 6.13
CAPTURE options, page 3.

H:MYTEST.TXT is being sent to the print queue called PRINTQ_0, and the banner name to appear on the cover sheet of the output is NANCY. After the job is printed, the printer will eject to the top of the next page in accord with the FF (form feed) setting.

SUMMARY

Command line utilities are different than menu utilities: CLUs are keyed in and have no menus. These commands can be entered at the prompt or can be put in a login script or a menu. Several CLU commands are similar to DOS commands. The commands are useful for daily operation of a LAN.

EXERCISES

1. Define the following:
   (a) inherited rights filter
   (b) attach
   (c) file attributes

```
┌─────────────────────────────────────────────────────────────────────────┐
│ NPRINT              General Help Screen                        4.10       │
├─────────────────────────────────────────────────────────────────────────┤
│ Purpose: Send files to a network printer.                                 │
├─────────────────────────────────────────────────────────────────────────┤
│ Syntax: NPRINT <path/filename> [options]                                  │
│ Options:                                                                   │
│  Delete (DEL)                                                              │
│  Job (J = <configuration>). You can also specify the                      │
│             context in which to look for a print                          │
│             job configuration if it is outside the                        │
│             current search path by identifying                            │
│             the container or user owning                                   │
│             the configuration:                                            │
│                  J = <configuration>:<context>                            │
│  Queue (Q = <queue name>)    Printer (P = <printer name>)                 │
│  Server (S = <NetWare bindery server>)                                    │
│  Details (D)                                                              │
│  Version (/VER) - Display program version information                     │
│  Hold (HOLD)    - Send a print job to a queue without having it print.    │
├─────────────────────────────────────────────────────────────────────────┤
│ Other help: Type  /?  or  /? ALL.                                         │
├─────────────────────────────────────────────────────────────────────────┤
│ > > >Enter = More  C = Continuous  Esc = Cancel                           │
└─────────────────────────────────────────────────────────────────────────┘
```

FIGURE 6.14
NPRINT features.

    (d) directory attributes

    (e) granting rights

    (f) trustee rights versus inherited rights

2. What do the following stand for?

    (a) CLU

    (b) CAPTURE parameters: B; C; FF; Q; S; TI; and NOTI.

    (c) FLAG file options: A; EO; H; I; N; NS; RO; RW; S; and T.

    (d) FLAG directory options: DI; H; N; P; RI; and SY.

3. Which CLU commands are similar to DOS commands?

4. Which CLU commands allow you to work with or view directory information?

5. Which CLU commands allow you to work with or view printer information?

6. Where are command line utilities located and who may use them?

7. What is the difference between command line utilities and menu utilities?

8. Which commands are used when communicating on a network?

LAB 6

The following lab will give you practice with using command line utilities. You are presented with different problems that are answerable using the CLUs learned in this chapter. Practice this lab periodically to increase your confidence in using CLUs.

1. Hide one of your files that is located in your home directory.
2. Set your entire directory to private.
3. Grant a friend read and file scan rights to your directory.
4. Find out how much space the volume SYS; has allocated. How much space is in use? How much space is still available?
5. Use the NPRINT command to print one of your files.
6. Find out the version of NetWare currently in use.
7. Write down the first two account names that appear on the list of users currently logged on to the system.
8. What is your station number?
9. What servers can you log on to?
10. Unhide any that you have previously hidden in your directory.
11. Display the rights to your directory.
12. Send a message to a friend.
13. Take away the rights that you had previously assigned to a friend in step 3.

CHAPTER SEVEN

PRINT UTILITIES

INSPIRING MOMENT

You are busy in your new position as a network administrator. You enjoy your job, but there is one problem. Users from various departments continue to come to you complaining about the printers or their printouts. Some common questions and concerns are:

"Where's my printout? I've been waiting a long time for it."

"Did my print job go to the printer on the first floor or the tenth floor?"

"How can I make sure my reports come out in sets of two and in condensed print?"

They all look to you for answers. Sometimes, they are very demanding and get upset when their printouts do not come out right. As a network administrator, you are responsible for maintaining the printers and coordinating the sharing of them. You want to keep the users content as much as possible. How do you make sure they get their reports and other printouts *and* ensure they are printed the way each user wants?

QUESTIONS FOR THOUGHT

If you were in charge of printing and output distribution, how would you set up your system to lessen the error rate? How would you inform the users of the procedures?

CHALLENGE

Once you understand which forms go to which printers, make a chart. Your chart should show the printer, print queue name, type of form, and other relevant information. File this chart for safekeeping; use a copy for reference. If you are in charge of users, share this chart with them. If you are in a situation where the printers are not working correctly and your coworkers are upset, remain

FIGURE 7.1
PRINTDEF's options menu.

```
PrintDef Options

 |Print Devices
 |Print Forms
 |Change Current Context
```

calm and try to rectify the problem. If necessary, call your supervisor for assistance.

OBJECTIVES

After finishing this chapter, you should be able to:

1. Discover the main purpose of PCONSOLE, PRINTCON, and PRINTDEF.
2. Walk through steps normally taken to set up and print a job using the print menu utilities PCONSOLE, PRINTCON, and PRINTDEF.
3. Explain how Novell NetWare makes use of print queues to print jobs.
4. Explore the options available for print configurations.
5. Explore the options available for printer definitions.
6. Define printer device modes and functions.
7. Explain how to specify different print forms.

EXPLORING PRINT UTILITIES

Three NetWare menu utilities—PRINTDEF, PRINTCON, and PCONSOLE—function together to allow a user to print documents.

PRINTDEF

The PRINTDEF utility requires administrative or equivalent status. It allows an administrator to identify forms and printer font capabilities. Normal endusers cannot make changes to PRINTDEF settings. The top user on the system is known as ADMIN, which is short for "administrator." The administrator can increase the power of an enduser account to be the same as ADMIN; this is called ADMIN equivalent. See Figure 7.1. PRINTDEF stands for "printer definition."

FIGURE 7.2
The menu used to set up printers.

```
Print Device Options
─────────────────────────────
  |Edit Print Devices
  |Import Print Devices
  |Export Print Devices
```

Print Devices

To choose a printer, first select "print devices" from the PRINTDEF options menu. Upon doing so, the "print device options" menu will appear. See Figure 7.2. Select the "import print devices" option.

At this point, the computer will ask for the directory location of the print device files (.PDF). The supervisor may specify a local drive's directory or a network drive. SYS:PUBLIC is the usual response to this prompt. Several .PDF files reside in the SYS:PUBLIC directory. The import print device steps are repeated for each print device file you wish to import. For example, HPJ4.PDF and HP3.PDF files could both be imported; the files are selected separately, however. A list of all .PDF files found in the specified directory will appear next. The supervisor should choose the one appropriate for the network's printer.

If for some reason the supervisor wants to change the .PDF file, he or she may do so using "edit print devices" from the "print device options" menu. To bring up the "print forms" utility, choose "print forms" from the PRINTDEF menu. A list of currently defined forms appears. Press "insert" to add a new form definition. The system will prompt the user for a name for the new form. After keying in a name, press "enter." Then the forms definition screen appears. See Figure 7.3. Enter the width in number of characters fitting across the page. The default is 80. Enter the length in number of lines of characters fitting vertically on the page. The default is 66. Press "escape" to save the form.

Edit Print Device

Upon choosing "edit print device" from the "print device options" menu, a list of imported print device definition files (PDF) appears. A user can then select the desired one, such as HP Laserjet 4 and press "enter." Then the "edit device options" menu appears. See Figure 7.4.

Choosing "device modes" brings up a list of fonts and corresponding pitches. Upon selecting a particular font/pitch combination, that particular selection's functions appear. Functions are coded lines that instruct the computer to carry out the font/pitch as requested. At this point, the administrator may make corrections or

FIGURE 7.3
The form definition function helps administrators identify forms by name and by number.

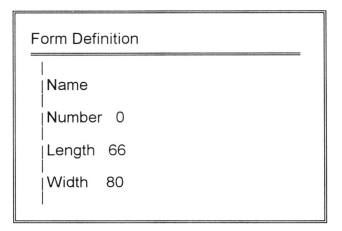

changes to the coded lines and press "escape" when done. This option is useful if the network's printer does not appear on the list.

New printers usually come with instructional guides, which usually contain a listing of escape codes for that particular printer. If a user does not find a .PDF file for a particular printer, it is possible to select a similar printer and modify the escape codes found in the selected printer's .PDF file. A user can change the escape codes to those listed in the printer guide for the printer in which no .PDF file exists. Make some modifications to an existing mode and function. This can come in handy if a printer manufacturer comes up with a new model. When a new printer is manufactured, quite commonly the .PDF file has not yet been released or for some reason is not available to the user. These files are printer dependent, which means that each file contains instructions for a particular printer's operation.

Change Current Context

If a user is trying to work with customized print device files rather than the predefined ones located in the PUBLIC directory, it may be necessary to change context to locate the files. To do this, choose this option and key in the context where the customized print devices are stored.

FIGURE 7.4
Supervisors may make customized changes to a printer's mode or function by using the "edit device options" menu.

Edit Device Options

| Device Modes
| Device Functions

```
 ┌──────────────────────────────────────────────────────┐
 │                                                      │
 │   Available Options                                  │
 │  ═══════════════════════════════════════             │
 │                                                      │
 │   │ Edit Print Job Configuration                     │
 │   │ Select Default Print Job Configuration           │
 │   │ Change Current Object                            │
 │   │                                                  │
 │   │                                                  │
 │                                                      │
 └──────────────────────────────────────────────────────┘
```

FIGURE 7.5
Customizing print configurations through PRINTCON.

PRINTCON

With so many users on a LAN, PRINTCON setups, which is shorthand for "print job configurations," vary depending on the needs of the particular user. Some users may prefer documents with tiny print; other users prefer large print. This utility allows a user to specify how he or she wishes to set up print configurations. Once into PRINTCON, the "available options" menu appears. See Figure 7.5.

Edit Print Job Configuration

To create a print configuration, choose "edit print job configuration." Press "insert" to let the computer know that this is a new configuration. The system will prompt the user for a name for the new print job configuration. The user would then key in a name and press "enter." Next, fill in the details for the particular configuration. The details required are fairly straightforward, such as "number of copies" and "form name." Form name, device, and mode require the same names used under PRINTDEF; pressing "enter" on these entries will bring up names from which to choose. To add names to the list, the administrator must use the PRINTDEF utility.

Select Default Print Job Configuration

It's common to have several print job configurations defined. For example, for some reports, a user may select a configuration that instructs the printer to print two copies of each report. Other reports require only one copy. Suppose a user sets up two separate print job configurations. Once the print job configurations have been added through the edit option, the "select default" option specifies the configuration that will be used most of the time. A user simply highlights the print job configuration name that he or she would like to set as the default and presses "enter." A small asterisk appears by the name denoting which configuration is the default.

FIGURE 7.6
PCONSOLE options.

```
Available Options
────────────────

  |        Print Queues
  |        Printers
  |        Print Servers
  |        Quick Setup
  |        Change Context
  |
```

Change Current Object

If the administrator would like to create a print job configuration for one or more users, the "change current object" option allows the administrator to specify which user or container (if for a group) to set as current. When "change current object" is selected, the system asks the administrator to enter a new object name. In this case, users and containers are considered as objects. Pressing "insert" brings up a list of users and containers from which to choose.

Using the Print Job Configuration

To invoke the print job configuration, use the CAPTURE command and specify the name that was assigned to the configuration:

```
CAPTURE J=MYPRINT
```

Note in this example that if the J=MYPRINT was left off, the system would use the print job configuration marked as default. If no configurations are marked as default, an error message would appear on the screen. The DOS TYPE command may be used to print once the CAPTURE command has been invoked:

```
TYPE MYFILE.TXT>PRN
```

Another way to print is through a word-processing application software. Anything that would normally go to a printer attached to the user's workstation would be redirected to the printer specified in the print job configuration.

PCONSOLE

PCONSOLE stands for "print console." The PCONSOLE utility allows users to see the print jobs currently in the queues and to add others. It is also used to add queues and print servers. When a user brings up PCONSOLE, the "available options" menu appears. See Figure 7.6.

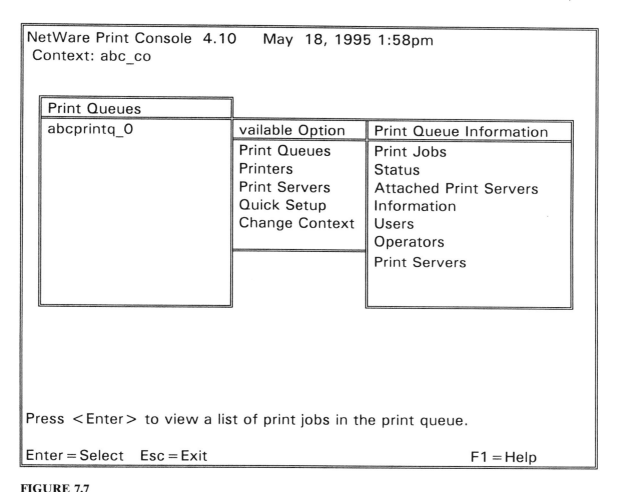

NetWare Print Console 4.10   May 18, 1995 1:58pm
Context: abc_co

Print Queues

abcprintq_0

vailable Option | Print Queue Information
Print Queues | Print Jobs
Printers | Status
Print Servers | Attached Print Servers
Quick Setup | Information
Change Context | Users
| Operators
| Print Servers

Press < Enter > to view a list of print jobs in the print queue.

Enter = Select   Esc = Exit   F1 = Help

FIGURE 7.7
The information screen for a particular print queue that has already been selected.

Print Queues

When the "print queues" option is selected, a list of defined print queues displays on the screen. A print queue is a waiting line for print jobs (requests) waiting to print. If a user highlights the print queue of interest and presses "enter," the print queue information menu appears. If the queue doesn't exist yet and the user is authorized to create a new print queue, the system will prompt the user for the name of the new queue after "insert" is pressed.

Print Queue Information

After a user presses "enter" on the particular queue of interest, the print queue information menu appears on the screen, as shown in Figure 7.7.

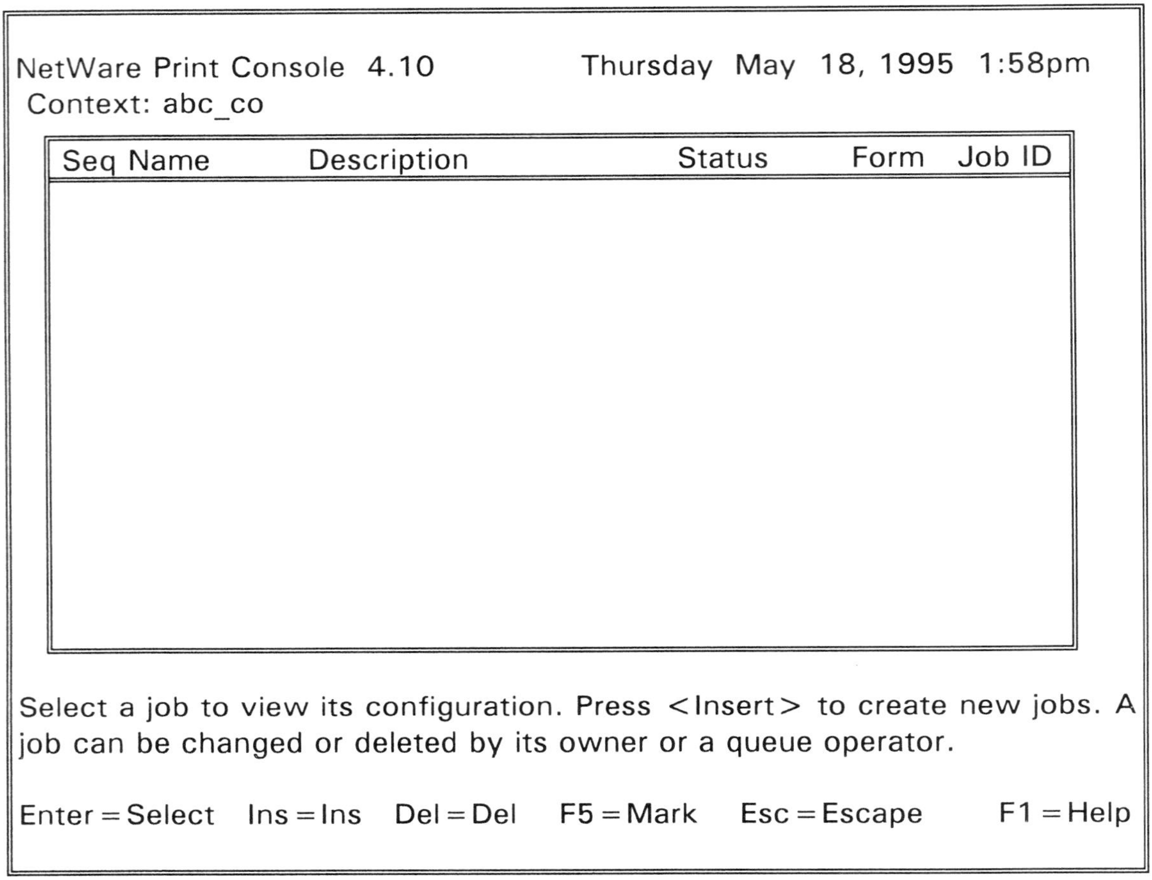

```
NetWare Print Console 4.10          Thursday May 18, 1995 1:58pm
Context: abc_co

  Seq Name       Description            Status       Form  Job ID
```

Select a job to view its configuration. Press <Insert> to create new jobs. A
job can be changed or deleted by its owner or a queue operator.

Enter = Select   Ins = Ins   Del = Del   F5 = Mark   Esc = Escape   F1 = Help

FIGURE 7.8
The "print job" menu shows jobs waiting to print.

By choosing "print jobs," a user can see a list of print jobs currently printing
or waiting to print. See Figure 7.8. When a user sends something to the print queue
for printing, the information sent, including the instructions noting how it should
be printed, is called the print job.

Specifying File to Print

If a user wants to submit a file to print, by pressing the "insert" key the menu
shown in Figure 7.9 will appear. If the user is not sure of the exact file name and
its path, pressing the INSERT key again will inform the network operating system
that he or she wants to be prompted. The first prompting screen is for the volume
name; see Figure 7.10.

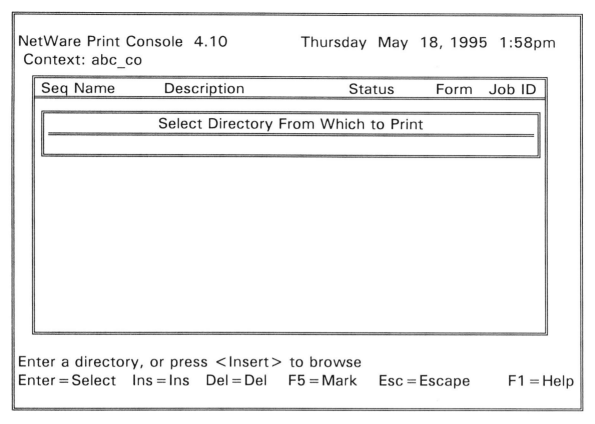

NetWare Print Console 4.10   Thursday May 18, 1995 1:58pm
Context: abc_co

Seq Name	Description	Status	Form	Job ID

Select Directory From Which to Print

Enter a directory, or press <Insert> to browse
Enter = Select   Ins = Ins   Del = Del   F5 = Mark   Esc = Escape   F1 = Help

FIGURE 7.9
In the "specifying file to print" menu, the system is prompting for the name of the file
to print.

After the user highlights the desired volume and presses "enter," the second
prompting screen appears asking the user to select a directory name. See Figure
7.11. Notice that if the chosen directory has subdirectories under it, the user may
be prompted to select a subdirectory name, as shown in Figure 7.12. Once finished
with selecting names at the directory level, the user may press "escape" and be
prompted for the file name. See Figure 7.13.

CHANGING PRINT PARAMETERS

Both the owner of a particular print job and the queue operator can change some
of the printing parameters. To view and/or change the parameters, highlight the
print job of interest and press "enter." The parameter screen appears; see Figure

```
NetWare Print Console  4.10            Thursday  May  18, 1995  1:58pm
Context: abc_co
```

Seq Name	Description	Status	Form	Job ID

Select Directory From Which to Print

Volumes

[Additional Volume Objects]	
[Additional Servers]	
ABC_SYS	(DS Volume Object)
A:	(Local Drive)
B:	(Local Drive)
C:	(Local Drive)

```
Press <Enter> to view the next level.  Press <Esc> to select the current path.

Enter = Next Level   Esc = Select Current Path   Del = Log out   Alt + F1 = More
```

FIGURE 7.10
Prompting for volume name.

7.14. The user can now make the needed changes and save them by pressing "enter." Changing the status of a print job is common. For example, the queue operator or user may change the status parameter to hold. See Figures 7.15 and 7.16. The user or queue operator may also choose to wait until a certain time before the job can print. This is done by answering "yes" to "defer printing" and specifying a date and time to print. See Figure 7.17.

If a print job is placed on hold, it will not print. When the hold is removed, by selecting "no" for this option, the print job would then wait its turn in line for printing. It may already be at the top of the line, depending on how long it's been on hold.

Status

Choose the "Status" option of the print parameters screen to view the current status of a particular printer. The status screen will let a user know if the printer

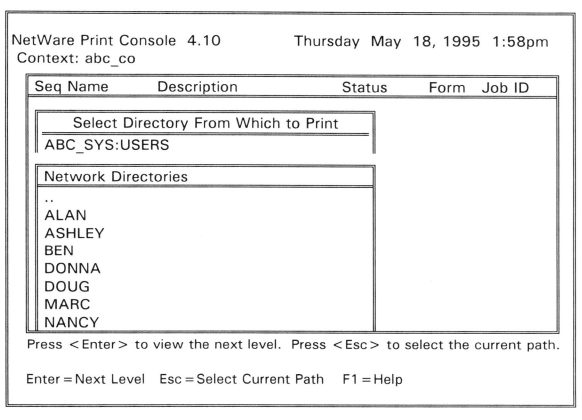

FIGURE 7.11
The select directory from which to print.

is "active" or "stopped." Sometimes the print queue operator has stopped the printer for maintenance or to change forms.

Print Queue ID

The "print queue ID" option presents a list of the print queue names currently assigned.

Queue Users

The "queue users" option provides a list of users allowed to use the currently selected queue. By pressing "insert," the administrator can add more users to the list. See Figure 7.18.

```
NetWare Print Console  4.10          Thursday  May  18, 1995  1:58pm
Context: abc_co

  ┌──────────────────────────────────────────────────────────────────────┐
  │ Seq Name          Description              Status      Form    Job ID  │
  │  ┌────────────────────────────────────────────────────┐                │
  │  │     Select Directory From Which to Print           │                │
  │  │ ABC_SYS:USERS\NANCY                                 │                │
  │  ├────────────────────────────────────────────────────┤                │
  │  │ Network Directories                                │                │
  │  │ ..                                                 │                │
  │  │                                                    │                │
  │  │                                                    │                │
  │  │                                                    │                │
  │  │                                                    │                │
  │  └────────────────────────────────────────────────────┘                │
  │ Press <Enter> to view the next level.  Press <Esc> to select the current path. │
  │                                                                        │
  │ Enter = Next Level   Esc = Select Current Path    F1 = Help            │
  └──────────────────────────────────────────────────────────────────────┘
```

FIGURE 7.12
The specifying subdirectory.

Operators

The "queue operators" option provides a list of users who have been designated by the administrator as queue operators. By pressing "insert," the administrator can add more users or an entire group to this list. See Figure 7.19.

Print Servers

The "print servers" option provides a list of print servers that the administrator has set up. Print servers, used in companies with many printers to manage, lessen the load of the file server by managing the printing resources. By pressing "insert," the supervisor can add more print servers to the list. See Figure 7.20. If a user highlights the desired print server and presses "enter," the screen that lists the printers for that particular print server appears.

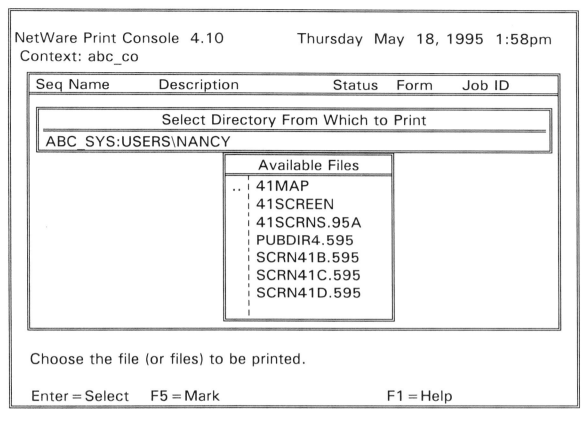

NetWare Print Console 4.10   Thursday May 18, 1995 1:58pm
Context: abc_co

Seq Name	Description	Status	Form	Job ID

Select Directory From Which to Print

ABC_SYS:USERS\NANCY

Available Files

.. | 41MAP
   | 41SCREEN
   | 41SCRNS.95A
   | PUBDIR4.595
   | SCRN41B.595
   | SCRN41C.595
   | SCRN41D.595

Choose the file (or files) to be printed.

Enter = Select   F5 = Mark   F1 = Help

FIGURE 7.13
Selecting the file name.

The Printer Screen

The printer screen lists the printers that are assigned to a particular print server. See Figure 7.21. Upon highlighting a particular printer and pressing "enter," the printer configuration screen appears. See Figure 7.22. On this screen, notice that the most common type of printer is the parallel printer; see Figure 7.23. Parallel printers receive data for printing at a faster rate than serial printers. Parallel printers receive data byte by byte, whereas serial printers receive data bit by bit. (Eight bits make up one byte.) Other types of printers are also available.

Service Mode for Forms

There are four options under "service mode" for forms: change forms as needed, minimize form changes within print queues, service only currently mounted form, and minimize form changes across print queues. See Figure 7.24.

```
┌────────────────────────────────────────────────────────────────────┐
│                                                                      │
│  NetWare Print Console  4.10          Thursday  May  18, 1995  1:58pm│
│    Context: abc_co                                                   │
│      ┌──────────────────────────────────────────────────────────┐   │
│      │           New Print Job to be Submitted                   │   │
│      ├──────────────────────────────────────────────────────────┤   │
│      │ Print job:                          File Size:            │   │
│      │ Client:                  Nancy[3]                         │   │
│      │ Description:             41MAP                            │   │
│      │ Status:                                                   │   │
│      │                                                           │   │
│      │ User hold:               No         Entry date:          │   │
│      │ Operator hold:           No         Entry time:          │   │
│      │ Service sequence:                   Form:          0      │   │
│      │                                     Print banner:  Yes    │   │
│      │ Number of copies:        1          Name:          Nancy  │   │
│      │                                     Banner name:   41MAP  │   │
│      │ File contents:           Byte stream                      │   │
│      │ Tab size:                                                 │   │
│      │                                     Defer printing:  No   │   │
│      │ Form feed:               Yes        Target date:          │   │
│      │ Notify when done:        No         Target time:          │   │
│      └──────────────────────────────────────────────────────────┘   │
│                                                                      │
│   Enter up to 49 characters to describe the print job.               │
│                                                                      │
│   Esc = Escape    F10 = Save                    F1 = Help            │
│                                                                      │
└────────────────────────────────────────────────────────────────────┘
```

FIGURE 7.14
The print parameters screen.

Change Forms as Needed The "change forms as needed" option takes print requests on a first come, first served basis. With this particular option, form changes would occur each time a print job requesting a form that is not currently loaded arrives to the top of the queue.

Minimize Form Changes Within Print Queues The option to minimize form changes within print queues seeks to have the printer process all the jobs requesting the same form before printing other jobs in the print queue.

Service Only Currently Mounted Forms The option to service only currently mounted forms allows only the jobs requesting the form that is currently mounted on the printer to go through. All other jobs are left waiting indefinitely.

```
NetWare Print Console  4.10          Thursday  May  18, 1995  1:58pm
Context: abc_co
┌──────────────────────────────────────────────────────────────────┐
│                  New Print Job to be Submitted                     │
├──────────────────────────────────────────────────────────────────┤
│ Print job:                          File Size:                     │
│ Client:              Nancy[3]                                      │
│ Description:         41MAP                                          │
│ Status:                                                            │
│                                                                    │
│ User hold:           Yes            Entry date:                    │
│ Operator hold:       No             Entry time:                    │
│ Service sequence:                   Form:           0              │
│                                     Print banner:   Yes            │
│ Number of copies:    1              Name:           Nancy          │
│                                     Banner name:    41MAP          │
│ File contents:       Byte stream                                   │
│ Tab size:                                                          │
│                                     Defer printing:  No            │
│ Form feed:           Yes            Target date:                   │
│ Notify when done:    No             Target time:                  │
└──────────────────────────────────────────────────────────────────┘
Choose yes to put the print job on hold.

Esc = Escape    F10 = Save                    F1 = Help
```

FIGURE 7.15
When a user places a hold on a print job, this screen appears.

Minimize Changes Across Print Queues   It is conceivable to have more than one print queue assigned to a printer. By choosing the option to minimize changes across print queues, the system prints all jobs requesting the currently mounted form from all the queues assigned to the printer before handling any form change requests.

SPECIAL NOTES REGARDING PRINTERS

There are many categories and types of printers currently on the market:

Laser printers provide clear output and can be used for heavy volume usage and fast printing.

```
┌─────────────────────────────────────────────────────────────────────┐
│ NetWare Print Console  4.10          Thursday  May  18, 1995  1:58pm │
│  Context: abc_co                                                      │
│   ┌─────────────────────────────────────────────────────────────┐   │
│   │              New Print Job to be Submitted                   │   │
│   │ Print job:                          File Size:               │   │
│   │ Client:                  Nancy[3]                            │   │
│   │ Description:             41MAP                               │   │
│   │ Status:                                                      │   │
│   │                                                              │   │
│   │ User hold:               No         Entry date:             │   │
│   │ Operator hold:           Yes        Entry time:             │   │
│   │ Service sequence:                   Form:            0       │   │
│   │                                     Print banner:   Yes      │   │
│   │ Number of copies:        1          Name:           Nancy    │   │
│   │                                     Banner name:    41MAP    │   │
│   │ File contents:           Byte stream                         │   │
│   │ Tab size:                                                    │   │
│   │                                     Defer printing: No       │   │
│   │ Form feed:               Yes        Target date:            │   │
│   │ Notify when done:        No         Target time:            │   │
│   └─────────────────────────────────────────────────────────────┘   │
│                                                                       │
│  Choose yes to put the print job on hold.                            │
│                                                                       │
│  Esc = Escape    F10 = Save                       F1 = Help          │
└─────────────────────────────────────────────────────────────────────┘
```

FIGURE 7.16
When an operator places a hold on a print job, this screen appears.

Ink-jet printers provide clear output but less volume usage than laser printers.

Dot matrix printers, which print letters made by forming small tiny dots together, are slower than laser and ink-jet printers and are not suited for high-volume printing.

To choose a printer, the volume of printing anticipated and the number of users that will be sharing the same printer must be determined.

```
NetWare Print Console  4.10          Thursday  May  18, 1995  1:58pm
Context: abc_co

                        New Print Job to be Submitted

Print job:                              File Size:
Client:                 Nancy[3]
Description:            41MAP
Status:

User hold:             No               Entry date:
Operator hold:         No               Entry time:
Service sequence:                       Form:            0
                                        Print banner:    Yes
Number of copies:      1                Name:            Nancy
                                        Banner name:     41MAP
File contents:         Byte stream
Tab size:

                                        Defer printing:  Yes
Form feed:             Yes              Target date:     5-19-1995
Notify when done:      No               Target time:     11:59:59 pm

Enter the date when the print job will be printed.  For example, "6 30 94"
specifies June 30, 1994 (6-30-94)
Esc = Escape    F10 = Save                              F1 = Help
```

FIGURE 7.17

The time deferment requested screen for changing print parameters.

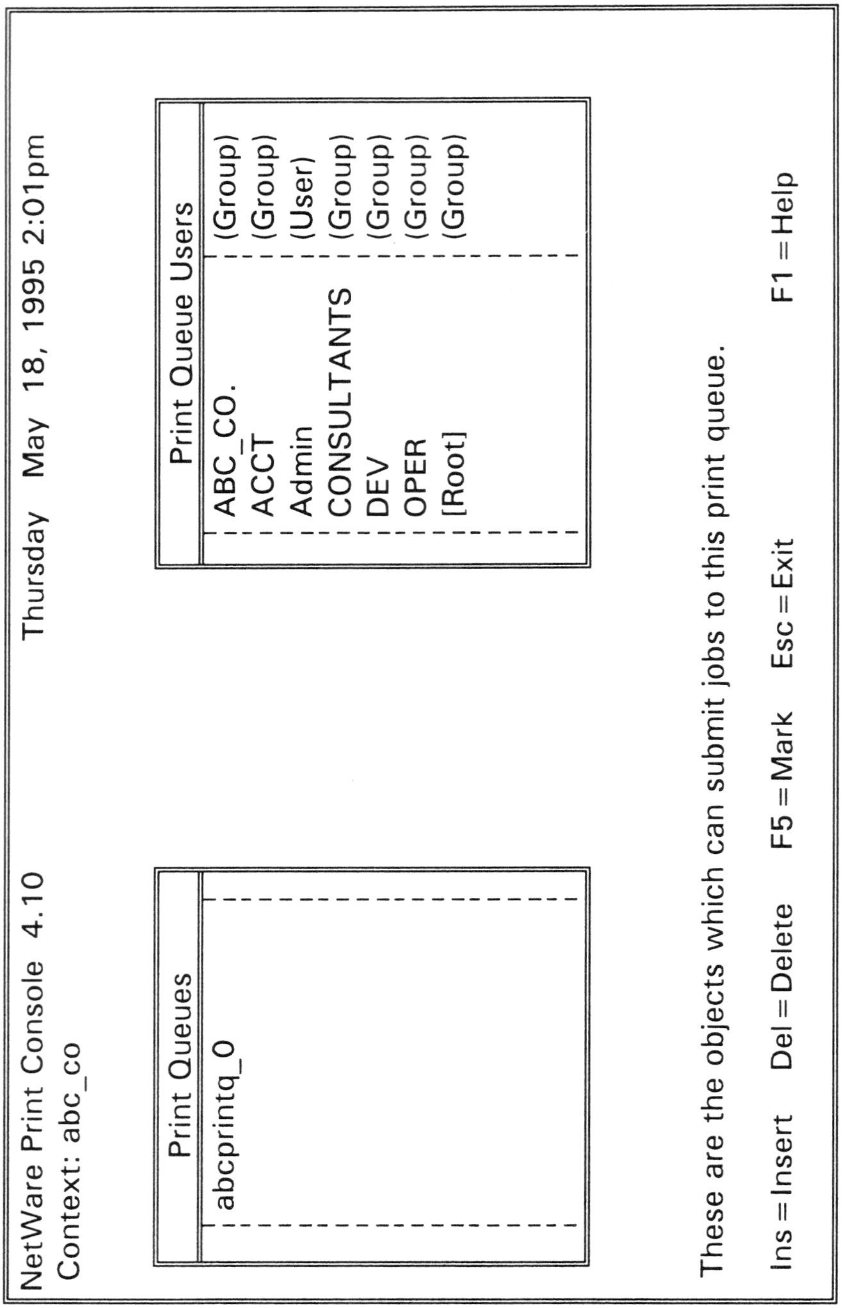

NetWare Print Console 4.10   Thursday May 18, 1995 2:01pm
Context: abc_co

```
┌─────────────────────────┐          ┌──────────────────────────────┐
│ Print Queues            │          │ Print Queue Users            │
├─────────────────────────┤          ├──────────────────────────────┤
│ abcprintq_0             │          │ ABC_CO.          (Group)     │
│                         │          │ ACCT             (Group)     │
│                         │          │ Admin            (User)      │
│                         │          │ CONSULTANTS      (Group)     │
│                         │          │ DEV              (Group)     │
│                         │          │ OPER             (Group)     │
│                         │          │ [Root]           (Group)     │
│                         │          │                              │
└─────────────────────────┘          └──────────────────────────────┘
```

These are the objects which can submit jobs to this print queue.

Ins = Insert   Del = Delete   F5 = Mark   Esc = Exit   F1 = Help

FIGURE 7.18
The "queue users" option.

```
NetWare Print Console  4.10          Thursday  May  18, 1995 2:01pm
Context: abc_co

  ┌─────────────────────┐        ┌────────────────────────────────────┐
  │ Print Queues        │        │ Print Queue Operators              │
  ├─────────────────────┤        ├────────────────────────────────────┤
  │ abcprintq_0         │        │ Admin                 | (User)      │
  │                     │        │ Ben.CONSULTANTS       | (User)      │
  │                     │        │ Marc.CONSULTANTS      | (User)      │
  │                     │        │ Nancy.CONSULTANTS     | (user)      │
  │                     │        │ Thomas.CONSULTANTS    | (user)      │
  │                     │        │ (Root)                              │
  └─────────────────────┘        └────────────────────────────────────┘

These are the objects which can manage the status of this print queue and its
print job entries.
Ins = Insert   Del = Delete   F5 = Mark   Esc = Exit          F1 = Help
```

FIGURE 7.19
The "queue operators" option.

NetWare Print Console 4.10   Thursday May 18, 1995 2:01pm
Context: abc_co

Print Queues   Print Servers

| abcprintq_0 | | PS_CLC   (print server) |

These are the objects which which have rights to service this print queue.

Ins = Insert   Del = Delete   F5 = Mark   Esc = Exit   F1 = Help

FIGURE 7.20
Print servers.

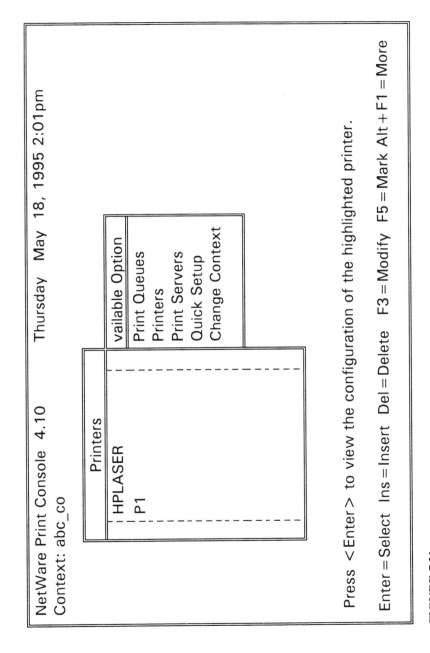

NetWare Print Console 4.10   Thursday May 18, 1995 2:01pm
Context: abc_co

```
        Printers
       ┌──────────────┐  vailable Option
       │ ┄┄┄┄┄┄┄┄┄┄┄  │  Print Queues
       │  HPLASER     │  Printers
       │  P1          │  Print Servers
       │              │  Quick Setup
       │ ┄┄┄┄┄┄┄┄┄┄┄  │  Change Context
       └──────────────┘
```

Press <Enter> to view the configuration of the highlighted printer.

Enter = Select Ins = Insert Del = Delete   F3 = Modify F5 = Mark Alt + F1 = More

FIGURE 7.21
Printer screen.

```
NetWare Print Console 4.10          Thursday  May  18, 1995 2:01pm
Context: abc_co

                    Printer HPLASER Configuration

      Print server:              PS_CLC
      Printer number:            0
      Printer status:            (unavailable)
      Printer type:              Parallel
      Configuration:             (See form)
      Starting form:             0
      Buffer size in KB:         3
      Buffer type:               Text
      Service mode for forms:    Minimize form changes within print queue
      Sampling interval:         5
      Print queues assigned      (See list)
      Notification               (See list)

Specify the logical number (0-254, inclusive) assigned to this printer.

Enter = Select   F10 = Save   F8 = Port Driver Name   Esc = Exit    F1 = Help
```

FIGURE 7.22
Printer configuration screen.

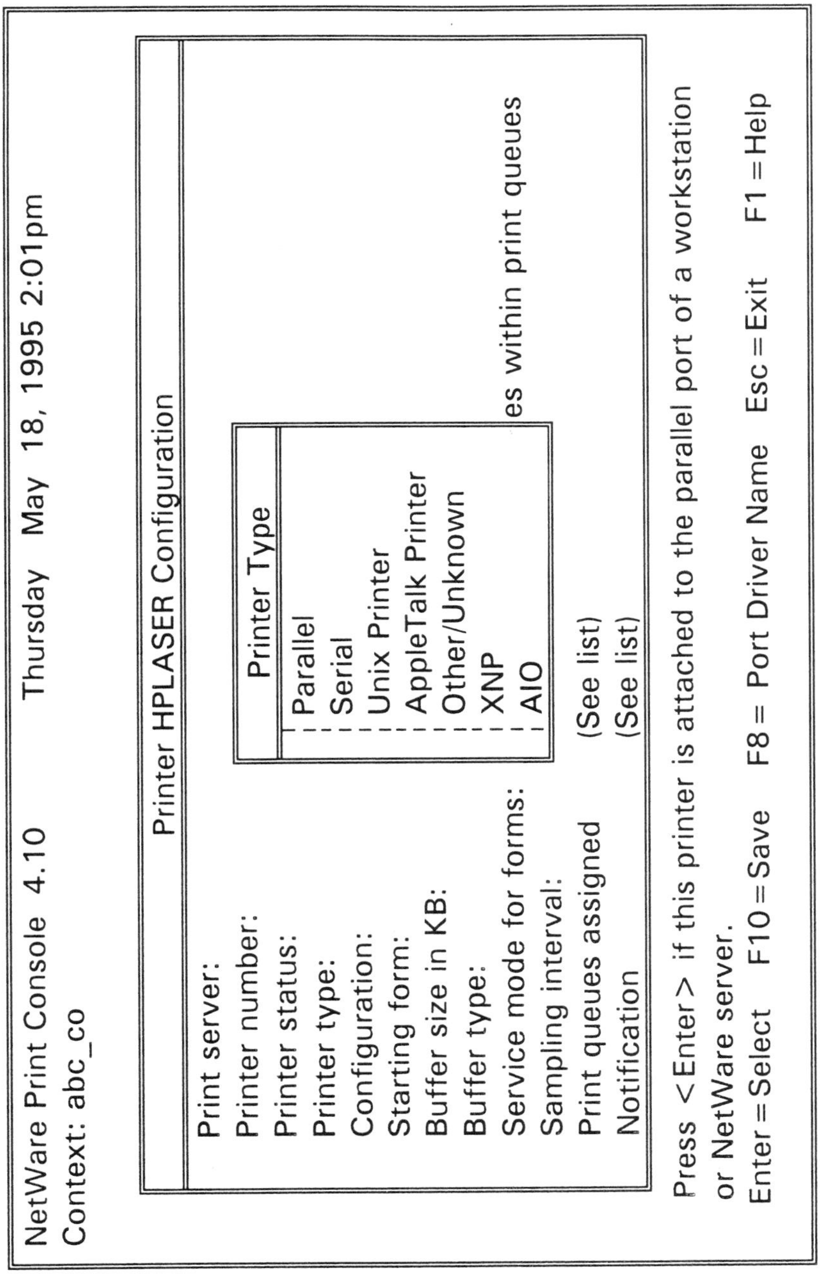

NetWare Print Console 4.10   Thursday May 18, 1995 2:01pm
Context: abc_co

Printer HPLASER Configuration

Print server:
Printer number:
Printer status:
Printer type: ┌─────────────────────┐
Configuration: │   Printer Type   │
Starting form: ├─────────────────────┤
Buffer size in KB: │ Parallel   │
Buffer type: │ Serial   │
Service mode for forms: │ Unix Printer   │
Sampling interval: │ AppleTalk Printer   │
                                      │ Other/Unknown   │
Print queues assigned   (See list)   │ XNP   │
Notification   (See list)   │ AIO   │
                                      └─────────────────────┘
                                      es within print queues

Press <Enter> if this printer is attached to the parallel port of a workstation
or NetWare server.
Enter = Select   F10 = Save   F8 = Port Driver Name   Esc = Exit   F1 = Help

FIGURE 7.23
Printer types.

```
NetWare Print Console 4.10        Thursday   May  18,  1995  2:01pm
Context: abc_co

                    Printer HPLASER Configuration

                              PS_CLC

                          ┌─────────────────────────────────────────────┐
                          │              Service Modes                    │
                          │ ┌───────────────────────────────────────────┐ │
    Print server:         │ │ Change forms as needed                     │ │
    Printer number:       │ │ Minimize form changes within print queues  │ │
    Printer status:       │ │ Service only currently mounted form         │ │
    Printer type:         │ │ Minimize form changes across print queues   │ │
    Configuration:        │ └───────────────────────────────────────────┘ │
    Starting form:        └─────────────────────────────────────────────┘
    Buffer size in KB:
    Buffer type:
    Service mode for
    Sampling interval:
    Print queues assigned         (See list)
    Notification                  (See list)

Press <Enter> to have the printers service batches of print jobs according to
their form in each print queue.
Enter=Select   F10=Save   F8 = Port Driver Name   Esc =Exit    F1 =Help
```

FIGURE 7.24
Service mode for handling form change requests.

SUMMARY

Three print utilities work together to end up with the final result: a printed document. PRINTDEF allows the supervisor to define printers and forms and make changes to fonts and pitches if needed. PRINTCON allows users to use the forms and printers defined by specifying job configurations. PCONSOLE allows users to monitor their jobs in the print queues and to add other jobs. It also allows the administrator to add more printing queues and queue operators and specify which users can use the queues.

EXERCISES

1. Define the following:
   (a) print forms
   (b) print device
   (c) form number
   (d) print job configuration
   (e) CAPTURE
   (f) print queue
   (g) print job
   (h) sequence
   (i) print parameters
   (j) operator hold
   (k) user hold
   (l) queue operator
   (m) print server
   (n) printer configuration
   (o) service mode
2. What do the following stand for?
   (a) PDF
   (b) PRINTCON
   (c) PRINTDEF
   (d) PCONSOLE
3. Explain and walk through what you as a user would do to add a print job to the print queue.
4. What is meant by *mode* and *function*? Under what circumstances might the supervisor make changes to the modes and functions?
5. What are the differences among PCONSOLE, PRINTCON, and PRINTDEF?
6. Explain what a print queue is used for.
7. A company wants to allow users to use three different forms: GREENBAR,

WHITE, and INVOICE. Which menu utility allows the administrator to enter the form definition? What information would the administrator need for adding each form? How should the administrator add these forms?

8. You would like to have two copies print every time. You also would like to print regular ASCII text files. How would you do this?

LAB 7

The following lab will allow you to gain experience with PRINTCON and PCONSOLE. After going through this lab, you may want to experiment by creating other print job configurations and using them.

1. Use PRINTCON to create a print job configuration. You would like two copies of your output. You also want condensed printing. For the form name, use your first name. Name the print job configuration GONOW.

2. At the F:\> prompt, invoke the CAPTURE command to let the computer know that it should use the print job configuration.

3. Use the DOS editor to key in the following text and save it as HELLO.TXT.:

```
Hello. This is a test of printing using a print job
configuration. This is only a simple test.
```

4. Print HELLO.TXT using the DOS TYPE command.

5. Print HELLO.TXT using PCONSOLE. (See print queue information.)

6. Go to the PUBLIC directory and locate PRINTCON, PRINTDEF, and PCONSOLE.

MANAGING USER ACCOUNTS

Part IV explores how accounts on a LAN system are set up. It also explores the security necessary to ensure that files and directories are accessed only to the degree needed for each particular user.

CHAPTER EIGHT

SETTING UP ACCOUNTS USING NETADMIN

INSPIRING MOMENT

After successfully working at a company for only a few months, you have been promoted to LAN administrator. It's Monday morning, and you are at your workstation and reading through your routine stack of notes, phone messages, and so forth. Suddenly you come across an urgent message from the Payroll Department. "To: LAN Administrator," it reads. "Our payroll data files have been sabotaged." You rush quickly down the hall to the payroll director's office. The payroll director announces that someone has been making unauthorized changes to personnel salary files. You discover that too many users have the rights to make changes to the Payroll Department's data directory. During your investigation, you discover that many users also have rights to change or even delete the company's customer database files.

QUESTIONS FOR THOUGHT

What would happen if suddenly all the customer files for the entire company got deleted? No longer could invoices go out to the customers. No longer could any correspondence take place. As a LAN administrator, you are responsible for setting up and managing user accounts. What should you do? How could this happen? Could it be a breach of security? Can incidences such as these be prevented? If so, to what extent and how? What would you do if data really did get damaged or changed? Would you hide the evidence? Would you start an investigation? How would you fix the problem? Could backing up the system help alleviate some of the problems?

CHALLENGE

When deciding on the appropriate rights to assign each user, think cautiously. Remember that users may think of how you set up their account or what rights you assign to them only if something goes wrong in this area.

Keep network documentation on what rights you assign to what user. Make notes (history file) of sabotages or other problems on the network. Only assign the necessary rights to each user. Remember that it's easier to give more rights later if needed than to clean up after a misuse of power.

OBJECTIVES

After finishing this chapter, you should be able to:

1. Identify and distinguish between ADMIN and user accounts.
2. Create individual accounts using the NetAdmin utility.
3. Assign trustee directory rights to the user accounts.
4. Explore Novell Directory Services (NDS) and what it means to choose a "context."
5. Identify how to change the context.

THE NETADMIN ACCOUNT

NetAdmin is a user menu utility located in the PUBLIC directory. To have access to LAN and maintain security, accounts are created. Without an account, a user cannot use an organization's LAN. To set up accounts, a person should have access to the ADMIN account or have been assigned ADMIN-equivalent privileges. In a class setting, this may not be possible. Students can view many of the settings to their own accounts, however, which should help the learning process. The only restriction is that students cannot change the settings.

LAN security is an important aspect of assigning trustee directory rights and setting up accounts. With proper training and care in deciding who should gain access to various parts of software and data, setting up and managing accounts can help a company or organization control and share resources on a LAN.

SETTING UP THE ACCOUNT AND VIEWING EXISTING ACCOUNTS

This section describes how administrators set up accounts on a LAN. Administrators are responsible for managing the overall operation of the LAN. Both ADMIN and ADMIN equivalents (another account status) have the power to create accounts. Users may find that this information clarifies how accounts are initially created.

The ADMIN account helps to maintain some source of control in the LAN environment. It is wise not to allow everyone access to this account; the more people with access to the administrator account, the more likely it is that the LAN will become harder to manage and control. The ADMIN account is created automatically when Novell NetWare is first installed. It is intended to allow one or two people the authority to oversee all aspects of the LAN. (If you do not have administrator privileges, log in to your user account. Because each location has different procedures for logging in, contact your LAN administrator, manager, or instructor for help.)

```
NetAdmin 4.55              Thursday  May  18, 1995  1:53pm
Context: CONSULTANTS.abc_co
Login Name: Nancy.CONSULTANTS.abc_co

                 ┌─────────────────────────────────────┐
                 │     NetAdmin Options                 │
                 ├─────────────────────────────────────┤
                 │     Manage Objects                   │
                 │     Manage according to search       │
                 │     pattern                          │
                 │     Change context                   │
                 │     Search                           │
                 └─────────────────────────────────────┘
```

FIGURE 8.1
NetAdmin options.

First, the administrator would log into his or her account. ADMIN is an account name, but unlike a regular user account, the administrator account has more privileges assigned to it.

After logging into the LAN, the administrator runs a menu utility called NetAdmin, which stands for "network administration." In configuring (or setting up) accounts one at a time, NetAdmin is ideal. Because of its menu-style orientation (see Figure 8.1), it is easy to use.

PLACEMENT OF USER ACCOUNTS

Before creating user accounts, the administrator must first decide where in the Novell Directory Services (NDS) the users should be located. This is considered by Novell as a "must do" first step and is part of the planning of the NDS tree structure. The users on the system are considered "leaf objects." It is important to decide the context under which the new account will be set up. For example, is the new user a member of a particular organization and department? Rushing through this section too quickly could result in a user who works in one department, say, the development and planning department (.DEV.ABC_CO), getting an account accidentally set up in the operations department (.OPER.ABC_CO). Figure 8.2 shows one company's organizational chart.

MANAGING OBJECTS

The "managing objects" option, when selected from NetAdmin's main menu, brings up the object, class screen and allows a user to take a closer look at the NDS tree. As shown in Figure 8.3, it is common to have the server named after the organization

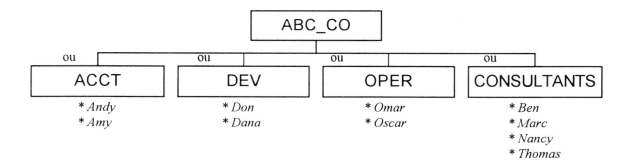

Context: Know the layout of your organization.
Under which Organizational Unit does each user go?

Note: Organizational Units are also known as containers.
User Objects are also known as leaf objects (that go inside
containers).

FIGURE 8.2
An organizational chart.

itself. The SYS volume, actually named ABC_SYS, contains the files and directories that will be used across the network. Notice that the print queue (the waiting line for printing), abcprintq_0, is also located in the root.

The administrator account, Admin, is also located in the root. Admin is an account created automatically by the system when the Novell NetWare operating system is first installed. The hypothetical company examined in this chapter is organized into departments. Each department (including outside consultants) is listed as an organizational unit in Figure 8.3. The object, class screen provides an easy way to view the organization's network structure. As the organization's network structure changes, the object, class screen will also change. Items may be added by pressing "insert" and then answering a series of questions. Items may be removed by pressing "delete." Maintaining the object, class screen is one duty of a network administrator. As disk drives, departments, or users are added physically to the organization, the network administrator needs to provide the proper information to the network operating system (in this case, Novell NetWare).

By highlighting the word "parent," located in the top right corner of the screen in Figure 8.3, the organization's network's NDS structure can be viewed level by level. The top left side of the screen indicates that the next level above is the parent or is a level above the current object. The current context is displayed in the upper left corner of the NetAdmin screen. Also displayed is the login name

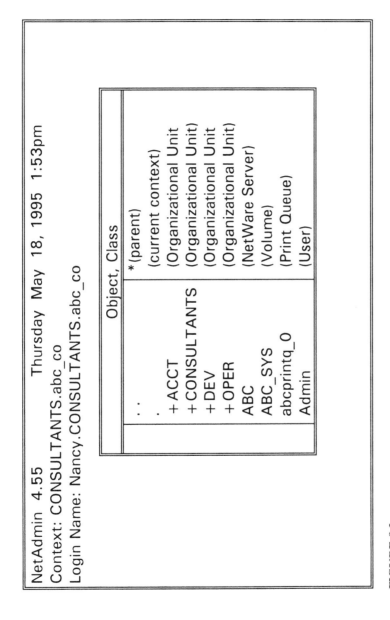

FIGURE 8.3

The object, class screen of NetAdmin.

```
┌─────────────────────────────────────────────────────────────────────┐
│ NetAdmin  4.55              Thursday  May  18, 1995  1:53pm           │
│ Context: CONSULTANTS.abc_co                                           │
│ Login Name: Nancy.CONSULTANTS.abc_co                                  │
│                                                                       │
│            ┌────────────────────────────────────┐                    │
│            │        NetAdmin Options             │                    │
│            ├────────────────────────────────────┤                    │
│            │  Manage Objects                     │                    │
│            │  Manage according to search         │                    │
│            │  pattern                            │                    │
│            │  Change context                     │                    │
│            │  Search                             │                    │
│            └────────────────────────────────────┘                    │
│  ┌─────────────────────────────────────────────────────────────────┐ │
│  │ Enter context: .consultants.abc_co                              │ │
│  └─────────────────────────────────────────────────────────────────┘ │
│                                                                       │
│                                                                       │
│  Type the context you want or press <Insert> to browse for the context│
│                                                                       │
│  Enter = Change context   Esc = Exit   Ins = Browse for objects  F1 = Help │
└─────────────────────────────────────────────────────────────────────┘
```

FIGURE 8.4
Entering the context.

for the user currently logged in. Recall from Chapter 1 that organizational units are used to represent departments. Organizational units are also called containers because the "leaf objects" are placed inside them. In this example, the organization (O=) ABC Company (ABC_CO) has three main departments: accounting, development and planning, and operations (see Figure 8.2). Users are located in each department; that is, they are located in organizational units.

CHANGING THE CONTEXT

Any time a user wants to change the context (for example, to work with a different department), the "change context" option from the main menu of NETADMIN (see Figure 8.1) should be chosen. Before creating a new user account, let's view an already existing one. In this example, "consultants" is the organizational unit (under the organization called ABC_CO). For the new context, enter CONSULTANTS.ABC_CO. See Figure 8.4.

SELECTING THE OBJECT

The next step is to select the actual user object with which to work. From the NetAdmin menu, the administrator or manager selects the "manage objects" sub-menu from the available topics menu. This submenu allows the administrator to

```
NetAdmin  4.55              Thursday  May  18, 1995  1:53pm
Context: CONSULTANTS.abc_co
Login Name: Nancy.CONSULTANTS.abc_co

    ┌──────────────────────────────────────────────────────┐
    │                    Object, Class                     │
    ├──────────────────────────┬───────────────────────────┤
    │      . .                 │   (parent)                │
    │      .                   │   (current context)       │
    │      Ben                 │   (User)                  │
    │      Marc                │   (User)                  │
    │      Nancy               │   (User)                  │
    │      Thomas              │   (User)                  │
    │                          │                           │
    │                          │                           │
    └──────────────────────────┴───────────────────────────┘

Press <F10> to select the parent object, <Enter> to change the context.
```

FIGURE 8.5
Object, class screen.

create or make changes to a user account. It also allows users to view information regarding their own personal accounts. When "manage objects" is selected, the object, class screen appears. Pressing "enter" while highlighting a container object (in this case, an organizational unit) shows the next level of the network structure. Here the move was from the root to the organization unit for the consultants. Notice that users are normally located inside a container. These user accounts are known as leaf objects.

The "object, class" screen appears (Figure 8.5), which shows the contents of the container for consultants. At this point, the object NANCY is selected. To select a user, highlight an object name and press "enter." The "actions for users" menu appears.

ACTIONS FOR USER MENU

The actions menu, as shown in Figure 8.6, allows users to view how their accounts are set up. This menu gives users some idea about what they can and cannot do. This section explores some of the "actions for user" options.

```
┌─────────────────────────────────────────────────────────────────────┐
│  NetAdmin  4.55            Thursday  May  18, 1995  1:53pm            │
│  Context: CONSULTANTS.abc_co                                          │
│  Login Name: Nancy.CONSULTANTS.abc_co                                 │
│    ┌───────────────────────────────────────────────────────┐         │
│    │            Actions for User: nancy                     │         │
│    ├───────────────────────────────────────────────────────┤         │
│    │   View or edit properties of this object              │         │
│    │   Rename                                              │         │
│    │   Move                                                │         │
│    │   Delete                                              │         │
│    │   View or edit rights to files and directories        │         │
│    │   View or edit the trustees of this object            │         │
│    └───────────────────────────────────────────────────────┘         │
│                                                                       │
│                                                                       │
│  Press <Enter> to edit the properties of this object.                 │
│                                                                       │
│  Enter = Select       Esc = Escape                    F1 = Help       │
│                                                                       │
└─────────────────────────────────────────────────────────────────────┘
```

FIGURE 8.6

Viewing or Editing Rights to Files and Directories

The view or edit rights to files or directories selection is used to determine which directories and files a user is allowed to access and to what extent the directory or file may be used. A user who is allowed access to a directory or file is called a *trustee* of that directory or file. The privileges assigned to the user that indicate the extent to which he or she can use the file are called *rights*. When this selection is chosen, the user is prompted for the "volume object name" (see Figure 8.7). As discussed in Chapter 1, the file server's hard drive has one or more volumes containing NetWare software directories such as PUBLIC, SYSTEM, MAIL, LOGIN, and ETC. The volume also contains software applications and data that users may be sharing. Notice in Figure 8.7 that ABC_SYS is the name of the volume on the file server. Also, notice that a period is keyed in after the volume object name "ABC_SYS." After keying in the volume name and pressing "enter," the right to files and directory screen reappears. Press the F10 function key (display list). The user's trustee directory rights screen now appears (see Figure 8.7).

Notice that this account does not have any rights assigned. This account does not need any rights assigned to it because it is set up as an ADMIN-equivalent account. ADMIN and ADMIN-equivalent user accounts do not need special permission to access directories and files; they have full reign of the system.

```
NetAdmin  4.55          Thursday  May  18, 1995  1:53pm
Context: CONSULTANTS.abc_co
Login Name: Nancy.CONSULTANTS.abc_co

                  Actions for User: Nancy


              Rights to files and/or directories

         Volume object name        ABC_SYS.::
         Beginning Path:
         Directories/Files:        Directory
         Trustee Search Depth:     All subdirectories

                                 Trustee directory, rights


                              (Empty List)




Press <Enter> to view/edit; <F5> to mark multiple; <Insert> to add.

Enter = Accept     F5 = Mark    Ins = Add    Del = Delete  Esc = Exit    F1 = Help
```

FIGURE 8.7
Rights to files and directories screen.

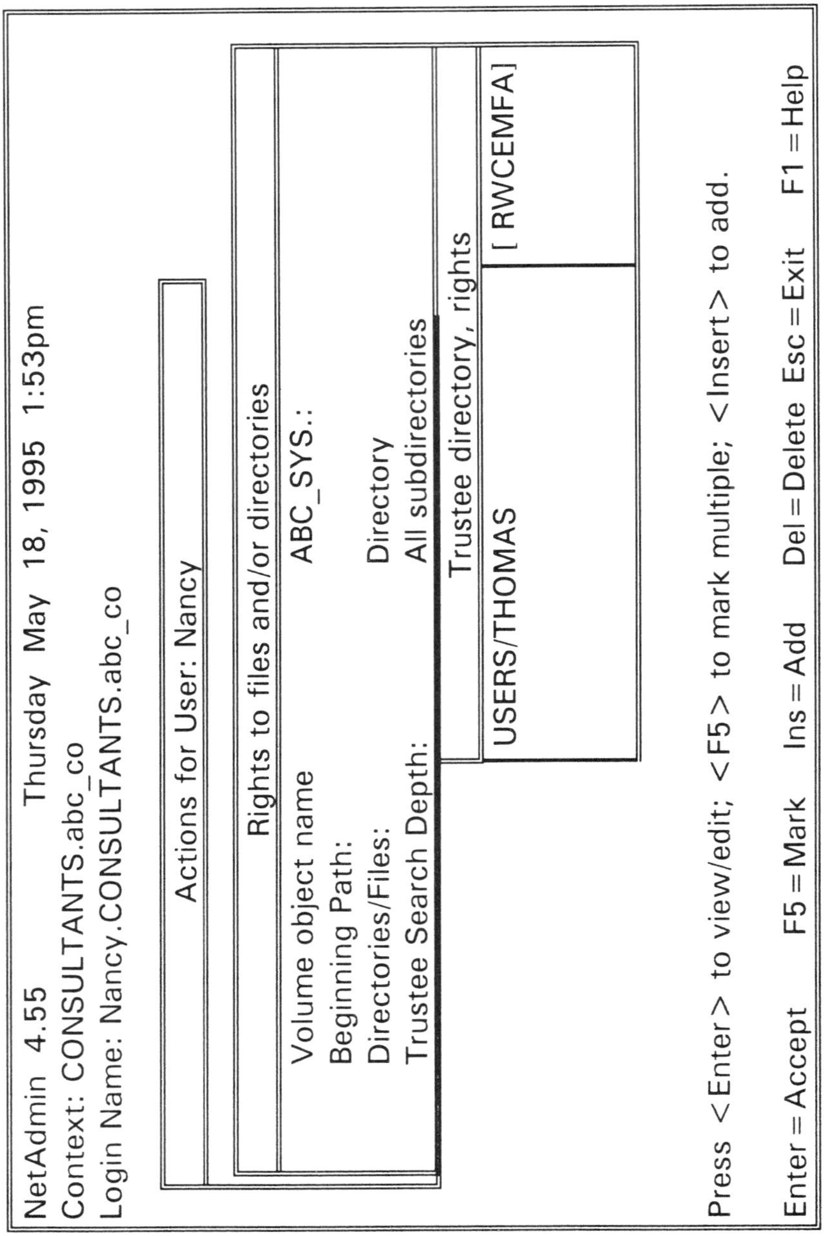

NetAdmin 4.55   Thursday May 18, 1995   1:53pm
Context: CONSULTANTS.abc_co
Login Name: Nancy.CONSULTANTS.abc_co

```
Actions for User: Nancy

        Rights to files and/or directories

Volume object name           ABC_SYS.:
Beginning Path:
Directories/Files:                    Directory
Trustee Search Depth:         All subdirectories

                      Trustee directory, rights

USERS/THOMAS                            [ RWCEMFA]
```

Press <Enter> to view/edit; <F5> to mark multiple; <Insert> to add.

Enter = Accept   F5 = Mark   Ins = Add   Del = Delete   Esc = Exit   F1 = Help

FIGURE 8.8
Trustee directory for Thomas's account.

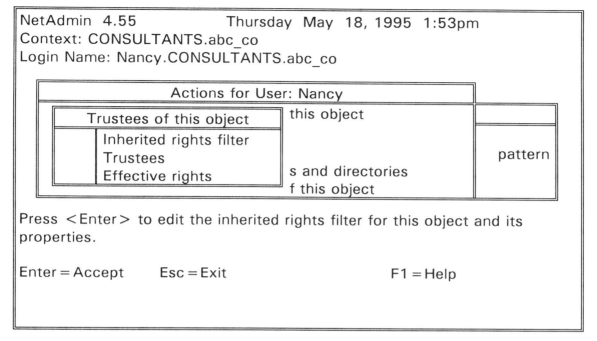

NetAdmin 4.55   Thursday May 18, 1995 1:53pm
Context: CONSULTANTS.abc_co
Login Name: Nancy.CONSULTANTS.abc_co

Actions for User: Nancy

Trustees of this object   this object

Inherited rights filter
Trustees   pattern
Effective rights   s and directories
                               f this object

Press <Enter> to edit the inherited rights filter for this object and its
properties.

Enter = Accept   Esc = Exit   F1 = Help

FIGURE 8.9
Trustees of this object screen.

Let's look at another user account to get a better idea of directory and file trustee rights. Go back to "manage objects" and choose a user account called "Thomas." Notice that after going through the same steps for the user named "Thomas," the trustee directory, rights screen appears (see Figure 8.8). All the directories or files to which a user has rights are listed on the left side of the screen. In this example, the directory is USERS/THOMAS. On the right side of the screen, [RWCEMFA] indicates that user Thomas has read, write, create, erase, modify, file scan, and access control rights to the directory. (This particular directory, located under USERS, is known as a home directory. It's a private directory containing the user's personal files and directories.) Notice in Figure 8.8 that this user has an entry that appears on the trustee, directory rights screen. Each user is entrusted to use certain files or directories. The administrator or person with supervisory or access control rights can assign trustee rights to users. Refer back to Chapter 3 for a description of available rights.

Viewing or Editing the Trustee of This Object

From the trustees of this object menu, there are three available options: inherited rights filters, trustees, and effective rights (see Figure 8.9). The following section briefly highlights inherited rights filters. See the RIGHTS command line utility found in Chapter 6 for more information.

```
NetAdmin  4.55                          Thursday  May  18, 1995  1:52pm
Context: CONSULTANTS.abc_co

                        Trustee Assignments

This screen lists all trustees of this object and each of its properties.

You can add or delete trustees, or change the rights of any trustees that
are listed.

The list is organized by property, with rights to the object listed first.

Procedures:

   To add a new trustee, press <Insert>.
   To delete an existing trustee, highlight it with the arrow keys, then
   press <Delete>.
   To see the list of rights that a trustee has to a property, highlight it
   with the arrow keys and press <Enter>.
   To return to the Access Control menu, press <Esc>.

                        Property Rights

To scroll through additional help, use the down and up arrow keys.

Esc = Exit Help   PgDn = Next Screen   PgUp = Previous Screen   Alt + F1 = More
```

FIGURE 8.10
Help with rights.

Inherited Rights Filters If a person is given rights at one level of the directory structure, those rights also apply to any subdirectories below that level. Inherited rights filters, however, may block certain rights from trickling down to lower subdirectories. For example, user Henry has been assigned the read, file scan, write, and create (RFWC) rights to a particular directory called REPORTS. Under the REPORTS directory is a subdirectory called YEARLY. If no inherited rights filter (IRF) is applied to the YEARLY directory, user Henry will have the same rights (RFWC) to this directory. If an IRF is applied, Henry will have RFWC rights only if the IRF also has those rights.

Notes Regarding Rights

See Chapter 3 for the rights available in Novell NetWare.

WORKING WITH HELP

By pressing the F1 function key (help) while on the trustee directory rights screen, more detail regarding these rights appears (see Figure 8.10). Notice the directions at the bottom of the screen. Use the page up and page down keys to scroll through the help screens, and press "escape" to exit.

MANAGE ACCORDING TO SEARCH PATTERN

If an organization is very large and has many users, printers, or disk volumes, the search patterns screen can help locate information on a particular object. From NetAdmin's main menu (see Figure 8.1), select "manage according to search pattern." For example, at the search patterns prompt "enter object name," key in the name of a user, such as Nancy. At the object class prompt, choose user; otherwise, the computer will assume that you do not know which object type you are interested in and will look through the list of different types of objects before finding the user Nancy's account (see Figures 8.11 and 8.12).

In Figure 8.11, an asterisk signifies "all" possibilities. In Figure 8.12, we are looking for a user on the network by the name of Nancy. Some special keys are noted at the bottom of the screen. To make changes to a particular line, simply position your cursor on that line and press "enter"; this will put you in the editing mode. Once the screen is filled in, press the F10 function key to save and process the selections. To change your mind and abort and exit this particular search, press "escape."

The F1 function key provides further information about this screen. Because we specifically requested to find the user Nancy, when the object, class screen comes again, it will only have Nancy listed on it, even if other users share the same context as Nancy (see Figure 8.13). (Also see Figure 8.5. Notice that there are more consultants than Nancy.) To view account information for user Nancy, simply highlight the name and press "enter." Upon doing so, the actions for user menu should appear on the screen. From this menu, various details regarding the user Nancy can be found. For example, by selecting "rights to files and/or directories," it's possible to see which files or directories this user is allowed to access.

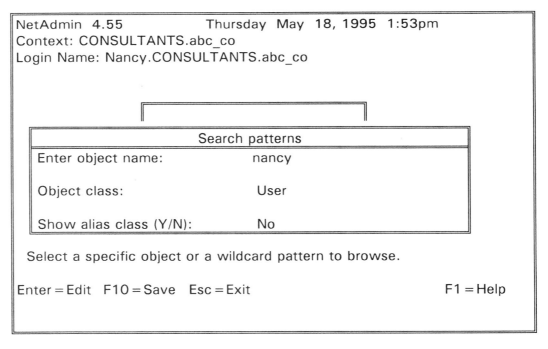

```
NetAdmin  4.55              Thursday  May  18, 1995  1:53pm
Context: CONSULTANTS.abc_co
Login Name: Nancy.CONSULTANTS.abc_co




                        ┌──────────────────────┐
          ┌─────────────┴──────────────────────┴────────────┐
          │                 Search patterns                  │
          ├──────────────────────────────────────────────────┤
          │  Enter object name:              *               │
          │                                                  │
          │  Object class:                   /All classes/   │
          │                                                  │
          │  Show alias class (Y/N):         No              │
          └──────────────────────────────────────────────────┘

     Select a specific object or a wildcard pattern to browse.

  Enter = Edit  F10 = Save  Esc = Exit                F1 = Help

```

FIGURE 8.11
Search patterns.

```
NetAdmin  4.55              Thursday  May  18, 1995  1:53pm
Context: CONSULTANTS.abc_co
Login Name: Nancy.CONSULTANTS.abc_co




                        ┌──────────────────────┐
          ┌─────────────┴──────────────────────┴────────────┐
          │                 Search patterns                  │
          ├──────────────────────────────────────────────────┤
          │  Enter object name:              nancy           │
          │                                                  │
          │  Object class:                   User            │
          │                                                  │
          │  Show alias class (Y/N):         No              │
          └──────────────────────────────────────────────────┘

     Select a specific object or a wildcard pattern to browse.

  Enter = Edit  F10 = Save  Esc = Exit                F1 = Help

```

FIGURE 8.12
Search patterns—object class—Nancy.

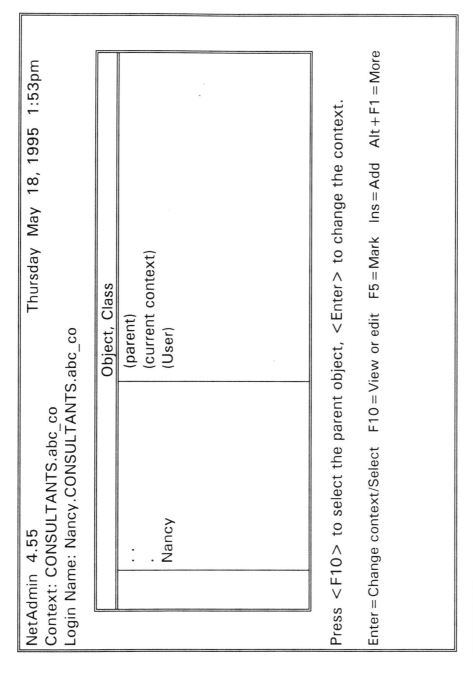

FIGURE 8.13
Object, class—user—Nancy.

SUMMARY

This chapter explored how to set up user accounts and manager group assignments using the menu utility called NetAdmin. To set up user accounts, administrator or equivalent authority is needed. A user may view the settings of his or her own account. Changing context allows a user to explore different sections of the NDS tree. The Novell Directory Services (NDS) tree structure is generally based on the company's own hierarchical chart. NetAdmin is also useful for viewing or editing file and directory rights. Trustees are assigned rights at a particular directory level. Effective rights consist of rights that have been assigned or inherited and have not been filtered out by an inherited rights filter (IRF).

EXERCISES

1. Define the following:
   (a) network administrator
   (b) print queue
   (c) SYS volume
   (d) container
   (e) leaf objects
   (f) home directory
   (g) rights
   (h) trustee
   (i) inherited rights filter

2. What do the following stand for?
   (a) NDS
   (b) O
   (c) OU
   (d) SRWCEMFA
   (e) IRF
   (f) *
   (g) NetAdmin

3. Briefly explain the difference between being an administrator and being a regular user.
4. What is the purpose of assigning trustee directory rights?
5. List the rights available with Novell NetWare 4.1 and the meaning of each.
6. Explain what a context is and how to change the context.
7. Why is it important to know the structure of the organization when setting up accounts?

8. Explain what is meant by organizations, organizational units, and leaf objects.
9. Under what circumstances might a person use an inherited rights filter?
10. Why is it important to know how to use NetAdmin even if you are not an administrator or manager?
11. If you want to entrust user Abel to the directory SYS:GROWTH, but you do not want him to remove any existing files, make any new files, or change any existing ones, which rights should you give him?
12. In which directory is NetAdmin located?
13. Explain how the help feature is accessed and under what circumstances a user might access it.
14. What is the purpose of the search pattern screen?

LAB 8

In this lab, you will use NetAdmin to view information regarding your user account and also the structure of your network's NDS.

1. Log onto the LAN and bring up the NetAdmin menu by typing the word *netadmin*. Write down the available topics that appear.

Available Topics (for NetAdmin)

2. Draw a picture of your organization's hierarchical structure. Make sure to identify where you fit into the structure.

---

3. Choose "change context." Key in your context (for example, CONSUL-TANTS.ABC_CO). Write down your context in case you need it later.

---

4. Select your account name and press "enter."
5. List the options available under "actions for users."
6. Select "rights to files and directories" for your account. Which rights does your account have? List the trustee directories and the rights. What can you do in each directory?
7. Press "escape" until you arrive back at the object, class screen. Highlight the line that reads

```
..    ¦ (parent)
```

and press "enter" until you are back as far as possible.
8. Can you find your account information by using the object, class screen? Walk your way through by pressing enter on the appropriate context items; do not use "change context." As you do this, draw a picture of your network's structure.
9. Does your network's structure match your organization's hierarchical chart? Explain any differences.

CHAPTER NINE

LAN SECURITY, SAFEGUARDS, AND TROUBLESHOOTING

INSPIRING MOMENT

As part of your new position in the Data Processing Department, you are responsible for responding to users. Users come to you when they have problems. All the users who work at this location have workstations that are connected to a NetWare 4.1 LAN. Recently, there have been several reports of breaches in security. In addition, users frequently ask you to help them with logging on to the network because they forgot their password. You have decided to educate the users on the importance of LAN security. For example, unsuspecting users may not realize that using their pet's name as their password may leave their account open to intruders. You now need to explore and learn more about LAN security.

QUESTIONS FOR THOUGHT

Why are passwords needed? What damages could occur if someone broke into the LAN? Could files become damaged or get erased? Why is it important to control how much access a user has to a particular directory? How can you minimize the chances of someone breaking into your account? How do viruses invade computer systems, and what can be done about them?

CHALLENGE

Even as you study and practice networking, get in the habit of learning about and practicing security. Never leave your workstation unattended when you are logged in. Be careful selecting your password. Notify the administrator if you see indications that someone has been in your account. Remember that your organization or company may count on you to ensure the confidentiality of files or directories.

OBJECTIVES

After finishing this chapter, you should be able to:

1. Identify restrictions that can be set through NetAdmin to limit user accounts.
2. Explain the importance of password protection.

3. Explain what intruder lockout means and how to use it.

4. Explain why it is important to monitor directory trustee assignments.

5. Explain the use of the password restrictions and time restrictions.

6. Explain why viruses are a threat to a LAN and identify some measures that can help prevent them from invading a system.

LAN SECURITY

LAN security can save a company or organization both in terms of time and money. Each year, companies lose money through corruption of software and data. Whether intentional or not, many of these losses could have been prevented by following the simple guidelines discussed in this chapter.

ACCOUNT RESTRICTIONS

Account restrictions applied to an account can help with a LAN's security. To access the account restrictions screen, follow these steps:

1. Access NetAdmin by keying in "netadmin" at any prompt.
2. Select "manage objects."
3. Select the user for whom you wish to restrict the account.
4. Select "view or edit properties."
5. Select "account restrictions."

There are five types of account restrictions: login restrictions, password restrictions, network address restrictions, login time restrictions, and volume/space restrictions.

Login Restrictions

Login restrictions such as account disabled, account has expiration date, and limit concurrent connections govern the logging in process.

Account Disabled The account disabled restriction prevents a user or anybody else from logging in. It's either set to yes or no. If set to yes, no logins are allowed. The account would become disabled under these circumstances:

1. If an intruder unsuccessfully tries to break into the account.
2. If an administrator chooses to disable it. For example, if a user was going on vacation, the administrator may want to disable that account for the period that the user is away from the office.

In any case, an administrator or manager can enable the account again by entering "no" at the account disabled prompt through NetAdmin.

Account Has Expiration Date If needed, an administrator could answer yes to the "account has expiration date" line. In this case, the administrator would be prompted for the date on which the account will expire. After that date, the user could not log in.

Limit Concurrent Connections To prevent users from working at more than one station at a time, an account can be limited to only one sign-on per account at any given time. If this option is set to yes, the administrator is prompted about the number of concurrent sign-ons to allow. This option is especially helpful if new users are on the system. Users sometimes forget to log out and may be logged in to a number of workstations before the day is over; thus those accounts would not be very secure.

Password Restrictions

Administrators can use many options to control password security.

Allow User to Change Password When set to yes, the "allow users to change password" selection gives users the ability to change their passwords. In departments where several people share an account, an administrator may want to set this option to "no."

Require Password If the "require password" selection is set to yes, a user is required to have a password to access a system. If set to no, a user may have a password, but it is not required. Also if this option is set to no, a statement will appear on the administrator's SECURITY.EXE report stating that a password is not required for that account.

Minimum Password Length Short passwords are easier to guess than long passwords. To make it difficult for intruders to access accounts, an administrator can require a minimum password length. In working with computers, it is recommended that passwords have at least eight characters; the default is five characters.

Force Periodic Password Change If the "force periodic password change" selection is set to yes, an administrator or manager would be prompted about the number of days to allow before prompting the user to change his or her password.

Limit Grace Logins If the "limit grace logins" selection is set to yes, an administrator is prompted to enter a number. This number specifies how many times the user can log in once his or her password has expired. Once the number of grace logins has been exceeded, the user can no longer log in.

Require Unique Password If the "require unique password" selection is set to yes, a user will not be allowed to change his or her password to one used before. A new password would be required.

Network Address Restrictions

Network address restrictions allow an administrator to specify particular workstations at which a particular user may sit. Before using this option, the administrator must know the workstation's network interface card (NIC) address. The following user command line utility (CLU) indicates whether someone is already logged in at that particular workstation:

```
F:\>NLIST USER/A
```

This will provide the address number. An address number is assigned to each NIC by the manufacturer. It's advisable for the administrator to sit down and log in at the particular workstation of interest (that is, the one that the user is going to be assigned).

To implement the restriction, select "network address restriction." Press "insert." The computer then prompts for the address.

Login Time Restrictions

User accounts can also be restricted by the amount of time or the particular hours that a user is logged in. That is, an administrator can require that a user not log in during a certain period. To do so, "time restrictions" are entered and viewed under the user information menu of the NetAdmin utility. Note, however, that this login time restriction only applies to the log in process. If, for example, the administrator restricts the user to logging in between 9:00 A.M. and 5:00 P.M., Monday through Friday, the user may log in at 4:59 P.M. and stay as long as desired, unless, of course, the administrator issues a clear connection instruction. Thus, the restriction only applies to logging in, and it doesn't kick the users off when they go over their allotted time.

Volume/Space Restrictions

Volume/space restrictions allow for limiting the amount of disk space a user can have on the file server.

DIRECTORY TRUSTEE ASSIGNMENTS AND LAN SECURITY

The process of assigning trustee directory rights was explored in Chapter 8. The number of directories assigned to a user should be limited to those that he or she will actually need. The number of rights to those directories should also be limited. These steps help prevent accidental (or nonaccidental) deletion or modification of files and information leaks.

PASSWORDS AND LAN SECURITY

In Chapter 6, the SETPASS command line utility (CLU) that allows users to change their passwords was discussed. Review the list presented in Figure 9.1 for some helpful rules regarding selecting passwords. Wisely selecting and implementing password-protected accounts helps keep a LAN secure.

VIRUS THREAT

What is a computer virus? Some programmers write programs that are undetectable by normal means such as the DIR command. Virus programs are called viruses because just as people can pass a biological virus to another person, these destructive

---

Using Passwords—Rules to Keep in Mind

1. Memorize your password immediately. Do not write it down; it may fall into wrong hands.

2. Do not use a password that can be found in the dictionary. Sometimes people use special programs that search through passwords in a dictionary fashion to try to break into accounts.

3. Do not use the name of people, places, or pets that are familiar to you. If they are familiar to you, they could be familiar to others also.

4. Longer passwords are harder to guess or figure out than shorter passwords. Pick a password that is at least eight characters long.

5. Mix letters and numbers together in your password. Such passwords are difficult to guess.

6. Always log out of your account when you leave your workstation. Never leave your computer on and unattended.

7. Change your password periodically. Avoid changing it so often that you have difficulty remembering your new password, however.

8. Users can change their passwords unless an administrator specifically sets up those accounts to disallow password changes. Once the password has been changed by the user, only that user knows the password. Although administrators may still change the password to something else, there is no option to show even an administrator what password the user chose. An administrator's screen prompts are a little different. When requesting a change of password, he or she is not prompted to enter the old password first, just the new one.

9. Check with your company, school, or organization and follow the procedures in place.

FIGURE 9.1
Rules for selecting passwords.

programs can be passed to different computers. The most common source for virus spreading is floppy disks.

A virus detection program should be run daily. LAN floppy disks should be protected to ensure that they do not become infected. (Make sure that the floppy disks are virus-free before write protecting them.) A 3½-inch floppy disk may be protected by leaving the notch found at the top of the disk open. A 5¼-inch floppy disk is just the opposite; the notch should be taped closed to ensure that it is protected. This form of protection is called *write protect* because the computer cannot change the contents by writing new data to it or removing data from it. Note that work disks containing files that the user deliberately wants to work with and change should not be write-protected. If the disk is write-protected when the user attempts to save to it, then an error message occurs.

Users and especially administrators should keep a log of .COM and .EXE files, along with their file sizes. They should check periodically to see if any file sizes have changed; file size changes could possibly signify a virus that has attached itself to the file. An administrator should watch the directories used, especially the LOGIN directory, and should check the file sizes of COMMAND.COM and LOGIN.EXE. Backups should be made routinely and viruses should be removed before running the backups. An administrator should monitor and inform all users of the importance of these precautions.

SAFEGUARDS AND TROUBLESHOOTING

A LAN administrator wants a LAN that operates efficiently and that does not crash. Although nothing can guarantee those results, the following tips may help.

Troubleshooting

Most problems involving efficient operation of a LAN in terms of hardware are associated with cables and connections. Cables should be checked for any bends or damage, and suspected bad cables should be replaced with new ones. Connections should be tight and NIC cards should be plugged in all the way. If there is trouble attaching to the file server, and an AUTOEXEC.BAT file is being used at the workstation, each command should be tried, one by one, to see if that is the problem. If after keying in IPXODI an error message appears, either the NIC probably has a problem or the IPXODI.COM file may not be correct. For a bad NIC, swapping it out with one from another workstation may solve the problem. If so, all the workstation files should be copied over or the workstation installation program should be run again. Check the CONFIG.SYS file also to make sure that the line that reads LASTDRIVE = Z is there. If all the workstation files load, watch the screen to determine this; if the workstation is not attaching to the network, the cable is probably either bad or not plugged in all the way. Also, make sure that the prompt at which the user is attempting to log in is pointing to a network drive. It should, for example, read F:\> instead of C:\>. To change to network drive F:, key in F: and press "enter." If all this fails, a technician should be contacted.

Uninterruptible Power Supply (UPS)

Because a file server has several workstations relying on it at any given time, losing power to it also impacts those stations. The files currently open on the file server's drive may become corrupted or may not get updated properly. To make sure that this problem does not occur, an uninterruptible power supply (UPS) should be connected to the file server. A UPS provides battery power to the file server for a few minutes so that the console operator can bring the server down more smoothly. If economically possible, UPSs should be connected to workstations that are processing sensitive data.

Backups

All volumes on the LAN should be backed up periodically. Although backing up takes time, it safeguards the software and data for future use if an emergency occurs. Every company should have a policy of keeping one backup on site and one off site. Some companies have a policy that forbids taking sensitive data off-site; therefore, it is wise for the person responsible for making backups to check company policy before making off-site copies.

It is also important to recognize that installing the NetWare software onto the file server from scratch usually takes longer than restoring the setup from a tape. A high-speed tape drive capable of backing up a large storage capacity is highly recommended for networks today.

SYSTEM FAULT TOLERANCE

Directories and files located in the file server's volumes are usually used by many people. Therefore, preventing damage to the files and directories is necessary. *System fault tolerance* seeks to do just that. It compensates for hardware problems encountered during saving (or writing) operations.

Novell NetWare uses SFT I as a built-in safeguard. Some networks go even further and have SFT II or SFT III.

SFT I

SFT I involves the use of a *hot fix*. If the file server receives an instruction to write something on the disk and does so, it will read it to confirm that the write operation was successful. If it was not successful (that is, if that area of the disk is damaged), the material that the server was trying to write to the disk is relocated to a different area of the disk. This is a hot fix.

SFT II: Disk Mirroring and Duplexing

In a network that has SFT II, two hard drives exist. The server writes to both drives identically. With *disk mirroring*, one controller card connects both drives to the main motherboard. With *disk duplexing*, each drive has its own controller card.

SFT III: Two Servers and Server Mirroring

In a network that has SFT III and two servers, if the file server goes down, the second server takes over automatically. This is *server mirroring*.

SUMMARY

Maintaining security, keeping the LAN up and running, and taking precautions not only help ensure a better system of operation but also help a company work more profitably. Administrators and managers have a duty to enforce security measures. Installing or upgrading safeguard measures such as SFT II and SFT III and adding a UPS may be a responsibility of the administrator or possibly the equipment support person of a particular organization. In any case, each user should be aware of the importance of security, should always operate under security guidelines, and should offer suggestions for improvement when called upon.

EXERCISES

1. Define the following:
   (a) account restrictions
   (b) login restrictions
   (c) password restrictions
   (d) login time restrictions
   (e) volume/space restrictions
   (f) concurrent connections
   (g) grace logins
   (h) network address
   (i) system fault tolerance
   (j) hot fix
   (k) disk mirroring
   (l) disk duplexing
   (m) server mirroring
2. Why are passwords important? List several tips on their use.
3. What kinds of restrictions can be placed on user accounts?
4. List some rules for selecting a password.
5. Why is it important to limit directories assigned and their rights?
6. What can you do to help prevent the spread of viruses?
7. What is intruder lockout?
8. Under what two conditions could an account become disabled?
9. What is the minimum number of characters recommended for a password?

LAB 9

In this lab, you will get first-hand experience at LAN security. You will explore the security of your particular account on the LAN. After completing this lab, you will understand what security measures have been implemented for your account. You will be comfortable with changing your password. You will also be comfortable controlling whether a disk is write-protected or not.

1. Practice changing your password. First, log in to the system. Key in "setpass." (If you get an error message, check with your LAN administrator.) You should be prompted for your current password. Key it in correctly and press "enter."

   Next, you should be prompted for a new password. Key it in and press "enter." After doing so, you will be prompted to enter the new password again to verify that you did not make an error when typing it in the first time. Notice that as you type, passwords do not appear on the screen.
2. Attempt to log in using an incorrect login name. Type "login superuser." Write down the error message that is displayed.

3. Attempt to log in to your user account, but use the wrong password. What error message is displayed? Do not do this step repeatedly; doing so could result in your account having an "intruder detection" lock placed on it.
4. Following the steps mentioned in this chapter, find out if your particular user account has any account restrictions placed on it. Write a brief description of the restrictions you notice.
5. Following the steps mentioned in this chapter, find out if your particular user account has any login restrictions placed on it. Write a brief description of the restrictions you notice.
6. Following the steps mentioned in this chapter, find out if your particular user account has any password restrictions. Write a brief description of the restrictions you notice.
7. Following the steps mentioned in this chapter, find out if your particular user account has any login time restrictions placed on it. Write a brief description of the restrictions you notice.
8. Following the steps mentioned in this chapter, find out if your particular user account has any volume/space restrictions placed on it. Write a brief description of the account restrictions you notice.
9. To demonstrate the use of write-protecting your disk to protect programs, get out a floppy disk, preferably a $3\frac{1}{2}$-inch floppy disk. Slide the write-protect notch, located at the top of the disk, into the open position. If you are using a $5\frac{1}{4}$-inch disk, cover the notch with a piece of non–see through tape. Your disk is now write-protected.
10. To demonstrate that the disk is truly write-protected, place the write-protected disk into the disk drive. Next, use the DOS editor to create a small text file and try to save it onto this disk. Since you are trying to write (save) to a disk that has been write-protected, an error message should appear on your screen. Write down the error message that appears.

    If the network or computer at which you are sitting had a virus, write-protecting your disk will keep the virus from writing to the disk as well.
11. Take out your disk and change it to be not protected. Now attempt to create a file on it using the DOS editor. Notice that this time you can successfully save your work.

PART

V

AUTOMATION

Once user accounts have been created, automation tools provide an added customization for the user. This part explores the creation of login scripts and menus as part of the automation process.

CHAPTER TEN

LOGIN SCRIPTS

INSPIRING MOMENT

Suddenly you find yourself faced with controlling part of the logging in process for the users in your department. Some users need to be reminded of various meetings that they are to attend. Some users require the setting of special drive mappings when they first log in. Some users are new and would like a menu to come up to prompt them about their selections.

In addition to helping these users, you want to provide a motivational thought for the day on the screens of all users as they log in. And, as they start their session, you would like the date and time to display on each user's screen.

QUESTIONS FOR THOUGHT

How would you accomplish this? How can a LAN administrator interact with the users and others most effectively to contribute to a smooth operating environment? How can new users learn to feel more comfortable in a short time working in a network? How can LAN administrators customize the login process to fit the needs of individual departments? Could setting up menus for each department and making them run upon logging in help standardize the way users access and use information on the LAN? Could greeting messages make the workplace more pleasant for users? Could opening messages keep users informed?

CHALLENGE

Login scripts provide a way to have an environment already set up each time a user logs in. Determine what tasks you do daily and ask other users about their routines. See if login scripts may provide a way to automate the tasks.

OBJECTIVES

After finishing this chapter, you should be able to:

1. Distinguish among the four login scripts available with NetWare and identify when they execute.

2. Create a login script using the NetAdmin menu utility.

3. Explore the use of the WRITE command to display messages on a user's screen.

4. Define variable replacement and make use of it in a login script.

5. Explore the use of the INCLUDE command for incorporating text files into a login script.

6. Explore the use of the DRIVE command for specifying the default drive.

7. Discuss the use of IF . . . THEN commands for conditional operations.

8. Explain the use of the EXIT command and how to execute menus upon exiting a login script.

9. Discuss how to execute internal DOS commands within a login script.

10. Discuss the importance of mapping to the PUBLIC directory in at least one login script.

LOGIN SCRIPT FILES

Login script files, as the name implies, execute upon logging on to a LAN. They consist of commands placed in sequential order, similarly to an actor reading a script for a play line by line. Login scripts bear some resemblance to the AUTOEXEC.BAT file found in the DOS environment. AUTOEXEC.BAT executes after booting up a PC automatically (provided that it exists on the disk) and also contains commands that are executed in a sequential order.

Four kinds of login scripts exist in Novell NetWare: container, profile, user/personal, and default. Figure 10.1 summarizes the properties of NetWare's login scripts.

Container Login Script

After logging on, the container login script executes first. An administrator creates the container login script. When executed, the system date and time are usually flashed on the screen, along with a greeting and any special announcements from the administrator. Then drive mapping will take place. Most institutions have search drive mappings set up, at least for the PUBLIC directory. The container login script runs if a user in that particular container logs in.

Profile Login Script

The profile login script executes after the container login script. In effect, it is a login script for a group of users. The system executes the profile login script if a member of a particular profile logs on to the system.

User/Personal Login Script

The user/personal login script executes after the profile login script finishes. The user login script is customized for a particular user. This user can create and maintain his or her own login script using the NetAdmin utility by following the steps given in Figure 10.1.

Container Login Script	
Who can create it?	ADMIN, ADMIN equivalent, user with administrative rights (read and write) to the organizational container
Where to go to create it	NETADMIN Select "manage object" Choose a container object Press F10 for the object, action screen to appear Select "view or edit properties" Select "login script"
Where is it stored?	NDS
Profile Login Script	
Who can create it?	ADMIN, ADMIN equivalent, or user with administrative rights to the users' containers that the profile login script is for
Where to go to create it	1. Create a profile NETADMIN Select "manage objects," press "insert," highlight "profile" for the object type, name the new profile 2. Key in the login script NETADMIN From the object action screen, select "view or edit properties," press F10, choose "login script" 3. Assign the user to the profile NETADMIN Select "manage objects," select the user, from the actions for user menu Select "view or edit properties," select "login script"
Where is it stored?	NDS
User/Personal Login Script	
Who can create it?	ADMIN, ADMIN equivalent, users with administrative rights to the container in which the user/personal account is located, the individual user
Where to go to create it	NETADMIN Select "manage object," choose the container object that the user account is found in, choose the user account, press F10 for the object, action screen to appear, select "view or edit properties of this object," select "login script"
Where is it stored?	NDS
Default Login Script	
Who can create it?	Software manufacturer Novell
Where to go to create it	Not applicable to users
Where is it stored?	Directory: LOGIN Filename: LOGIN.EXE

Figure 10.1
Four types of login scripts.

```
MAP DISPLAY OFF
MAP ERRORS OFF
MAP *1:=SYS:
MAP *1:=SYS:%LOGIN_NAME
IF "%1"="ADMIN" OR "%1"="SUPERVISOR" THEN MAP *1:=SYS:SYSTEM
MAP INS S1:=SYS:PUBLIC
MAP INS S2:=SYS:%MACHINE/%OS/%OS_VERSION
MAP DISPLAY ON
MAP
```

Figure 10.2
Default login script.

Default Login Script

The default login script executes if the user did not create a login script. If there is no user login script, the network executes the default login script provided by Novell. See Figure 10.2.

CREATING AND LOCATING THE LOGIN SCRIPT

Figure 10.1 shows the steps involved to get to the actual screens for keying in login scripts. Notice that the container login script runs for the user logging into that specific container; thus it is advantageous to separate departments of an organization into different containers. Having a different login script for each department saves the administrator time in the long run, especially if everyone in one department uses the same software daily. Having the same login script also helps the administrator set up the same working environment for the users in a particular department (container).

Profile login scripts are handy when handling cases where a group of people not necessarily in the same department need to share the same software or have the same environment settings. For example, the president of an organization may decide that all managers in the company need access to some sensitive data files. Because the managers are in different departments, a profile login script is needed.

User/personal login scripts allow customizing individual user environments. Any special features needed by certain people and not the whole department can possibly be handled in the user's login script. The container, profile, and user/personal login scripts are all created using the NetAdmin user menu utility, which is located in the PUBLIC directory. The actual login scripts created are physically stored in the network's NDS (Novell Directory Services).

The default login script may not be modified by any user. The default login script, unlike the other types of login scripts, is not located in the NDS; rather, it is located in the LOGIN directory and is built into the LOGIN.EXE program. Recall from Chapter 1 that LOGIN.EXE is the program that controls the login process. When a user keys in the words "LOGIN USER01," for example, he or she is instructing the network operating system to execute the LOGIN.EXE program. (Recall that if a program's file name ends with the extension .EXE, .COM or .BAT, the user does not need to key in the extension name.)

COMMON LOGIN SCRIPT COMMANDS

Several login script commands and examples of how to use them are now presented. These commands can be placed in the container, profile, or user/personal login script. As noted earlier, the default login script also contains a number of commands.

WRITE Command

The WRITE command allows messages to be displayed on the screen, as shown in this example:

```
WRITE "Hello There"
```

Sometimes a user may wish for a different message, depending on when he or she logs in. To accomplish this, NetWare has a number of variable replacements, which all start with a percent sign (%). Some common variable replacements are shown in Figure 10.3. The following list represents a few variable replacements; others are included in the documentation that comes with the NetWare software.

WRITE "Today is %DAY_OF_WEEK" to display the current weekday.

WRITE "The month is %MONTH_NAME" to display the current month.

WRITE "Are you a graduate of %SHORT_YEAR" to display the last two numbers of the year.

WRITE "%YEAR is a good year" to display the complete year.

WRITE "Today is the %DAY" to display the current date.

WRITE "Today is %MONTH_NAME %DAY %YEAR" to complete the date. Note that more than one variable replacement may be used on the same line.

WRITE "The time now is %HOUR: %MINUTE %AM_PM" to display the current time followed by A.M. or P.M.

WRITE "The time is %HOUR24:%MINUTE:%SECOND" to display the time in a 24-hour format.

WRITE "Good %GREETING_TIME" to display a greeting as morning, afternoon, or evening, depending on the current time.

WRITE "Hello %FULL_NAME" to display the user's full name. This is the same as that found under "user information" through NetAdmin.

WRITE "Your account name is %LOGIN_NAME" to display the account name, such as USER01.

Variable Replacement	Meaning Assigned to Variable Replacement
%ACCOUNT_BALANCE	Amount of funds remaining in the user's account.
%CN	Common name. This is normally referred to as the user's login name.
%FILE_SERVER	Name of the file server currently active for this user's session.
%FULL_NAME	Full name of the user. This is entered when the account is set up in NetAdmin.
%LAST_NAME	Last name of the user. This is entered when the account is set up in NetAdmin.
%LOGIN_CONTEXT	Login context to which the system is currently pointing in the NDS.
%LOGIN_NAME	User's login name.
%MACHINE	Type of computer, IBM-PC, for example.
%OS	Local operating system, for example, MS-DOS.
%OS_VERSION	Version of the local operating system in use by the workstation.
%PASSWORD_EXPIRES	Number of days before password expires.
%PROFILE	Profile name, if the user belongs to a profile.
%STATION	Displays the workstation's address.
%SURNAME	Displays the last name of the user as keyed in under NetAdmin when the account was set up.
%TELEPHONE_NUMBER	Displays the user's telephone number as entered under NetAdmin when the account was set up.
%TITLE	Displays the user's title as keyed in using NetAdmin when the account was set up.
%AM_PM	Displays either "AM" or "PM," depending on the time of day at which the user logs in.
%GREETING_TIME	Displays "morning," "afternoon," or "evening," depending on the time of day at which the user logs in.
%HOUR	Displays the hour that the user logs in.
%HOUR24	Displays the hour that the user logs in based on a 24-hour clock; for example, 1 P.M. is equal to 13.
%MINUTE	Displays the number of minutes past the hour when the user logs in.
%SECOND	Displays the number of seconds past the minute when the user logs in.
%DAY	Displays the date when the user logs in.
%DAY_OF_WEEK	Displays the day of the week when the user logs in; for example, Monday.
%MONTH	Displays the number of the current month.
%MONTH_NAME	Displays the name of the current month.
%YEAR	Displays the current year in four digits.
%SHORT_YEAR	Displays the current year in two digits.

Figure 10.3
Commonly used variable replacements.

WRITE "You are at station number %STATION" to display the station number.

WRITE "The local operating system is %OS_VERSION" to display the version of the local operating system, such as DOS, currently running.

WRITE "You are logged in as %CN" to display the user's common name.

WRITE "Your computer is a %MACHINE" to display the type of computer at which a user is sitting.

Sounding Alerts Command

The command FIRE PHASERS 4 causes the computer to make an alert sound four times. This is a good way to detect someone logging in to a particular account. The administrator may put FIRE PHASERS 4 in the container login script for the Marketing Department and FIRE PHASERS 5 in the one for the Accounting Department. From across the room, the administrator can tell if users are logging in to a marketing account or an accounting account simply by the number of beeps.

DISPLAY Command

The DISPLAY filename command displays text files. For example, by typing

```
DISPLAY SYS:PUBLIC\ANNOUNCE.TXT
```

daily announcements that the administrator has placed in the ANNOUNCE.TXT file located in the PUBLIC directory will be displayed. Users may wish to place reminders or project notes in a text file and then have the file displayed during the login process.

INCLUDE Command

The INCLUDE command pieces together login script files. For example, by typing

```
INCLUDE H:LOGSCRIP.LOG
```

the computer will process the script commands located in the specified file when the INCLUDE statement is reached in the login script. After that, control of execution will return to the line immediately below the INCLUDE statement.

Executing .EXE, .COM, and .BAT Commands

The #filename command is used to run a file that ends with .EXE, .COM, or .BAT from within a login script.

Changing Default Drives

By using the DRIVE G: command, the computer is instructed to change the default drive to the previously mapped drive G:. (Remember that maps are also permitted in login scripts.)

Conditional Instructions

By typing a conditional instruction such as

```
IF DAY_OF_WEEK = "Monday" THEN WRITE "Hello again"
```

the computer will check to see if the condition is true before performing the WRITE command. These conditional instructions are also known as IF . . . THEN commands. Notice that even though DAY_OF_WEEK is a variable replacement, the % sign is not used in the above example. When a variable replacement is used in an if . . . then statement, the % sign is left off.

Running Programs upon Exiting

The EXIT "NMENU MYTRY" command instructs the computer to perform the command that is in quotes upon exiting the login script. In this example, the menu MYTRY is executed. This command should be placed last in the login script. It is advisable to keep menu names short, no more than five characters instead of the standard eight, because no more than 11 characters are permitted between the quotes on the EXIT command. A menu called CUSTOMER would not run if requested within the EXIT command. If problems are encountered while attempting to run a menu using the EXIT command, the user may want to have the EXIT command execute a batch file and have the batch file run the menu. See Chapter 11 for more details regarding running menus.

Executing Internal DOS Commands

The commands #COMMAND/C TIME and #COMMAND/C DATE demonstrate how to run the internal DOS DATE and TIME commands. These commands work with any internal DOS command.

Mapping

Mapping, as mentioned above, can also be done in the login script (see Chapter 3). Remember that maps are not permanent, however, so by placing the MAP command in the login script, the mapped drive gets re-created each session.

SUMMARY

Login scripts, which execute immediately after the user logs on, make it easy to automate the execution of various commands. Four types of login scripts can exist on the network: Container, profile, user/personal, and default. A container login script is useful for customizing the work environments for users in the same department. Profile login scripts allow for customizing by other factors, such as job title. User/personal login scripts allow users to customize their work environments. The default login script, created by Novell, runs only if there is no user login script for the particular user logging in. Variable replacements help set up commands when missing information is not known ahead of time. Login scripts are flexible to allow for the running of DOS internal commands, NetWare menus, and other programs.

EXERCISES

1. Define the following:
   (a) login scripts
   (b) container login script
   (c) profile login script
   (d) user/personal login script
   (e) default login script
   (f) variable replacement
   (g) conditional instruction

2. What do the following mean in NetWare?
   (a) %
   (b) #
   (c) %AM_PM
   (d) %HOUR24
   (e) %OS_VERSION
   (f) %CN
   (g) %MACHINE

3. What are the four kinds of login scripts available in Novell NetWare, and who creates them?
4. When are login scripts executed?
5. Login scripts are similar to what command in DOS?
6. Where are login scripts created?
7. Where on the file server's drive are login scripts stored?
8. A map drive should be created in the container login script on which directory?
9. In what order are login scripts processed?
10. True or false: An administrator's login script is called a container login script.
11. What is the purpose of the WRITE command?
12. Explain what variable replacement is used for and what symbol precedes it.
13. What is the purpose of the INCLUDE and DISPLAY commands?
14. What is the purpose of the EXIT command?
15. How would you put the DOS directory command in a login script?

LAB 10

In this lab, you will create your own user/personal login script and will incorporate the commands discussed in this chapter. After completing this lab, you should be able to find the user login script screen and create a login script. You will also demonstrate your understanding of the commands presented in the chapter.

1. Go to the login script screen. Log in first. Key in "NETADMIN." Next, choose the container object in which your user account is found. If you are not sure

of your container name, ask the person who set up the account. Find your user name and press F10 to bring up the object, action screen. Select "view or edit properties" of this object. Finally, select "login script."

2. Key in the WRITE commands found earlier in this chapter. Each command should start on a new line and line up with the left margin.

3. Sound an alert using the FIRE PHASERS 4 command. Avoid putting a very high number on the FIRE PHASERS command; you do not want to alarm other users that much.

4. Use the DISPLAY command to display one of your text files on the screen. (If you do not have a text file yet, save and exit your login script by pressing "escape." Keep pressing "escape" or press Alt F10 to get out of NetAdmin. You may use the DOS editor to create a text file; refer to Chapter 2 for details regarding the DOS editor. After creating a text file, return to your login script screen following the instructions given in step 1.)

5. Ask your administrator or instructor if there is a login script file on the network that you may practice accessing using the INCLUDE command.

6. When you log in to the network, you would like the system to send a message to a friend automatically to announce your arrival. Remember that SEND is actually a program found in the PUBLIC directory; it's extension is .EXE. Therefore, to run it from a login script, you must start with the # (pound) sign. For example,

```
#SEND "Good morning, I just arrived." TO USER02
```

7. Create a logical drive map assignment to point to your home directory. Notice that even though MAP.EXE is a program located in PUBLIC, it's an exception to the rule regarding the # sign. The # sign is not needed with the MAP command. For example,

```
MAP H:=SYS:USERS\USER01
```

8. Add some daily motivational messages to your login script. Here are some examples:

```
IF DAY_OF_WEEK = "Monday" THEN WRITE "This is a great
week!"
IF DAY_OF_WEEK = "Tuesday" THEN WRITE "Reach new heights!"
IF DAY_OF_WEEK = "Wednesday" THEN WRITE "Go Go Go Go!"
IF DAY_OF_WEEK = "Thursday" THEN WRITE "I am confident!"
IF DAY_OF_WEEK = "Friday" THEN WRITE "Get to work!!!"
IF DAY_OF_WEEK = "Saturday" THEN WRITE "Take a rest!"
IF DAY_OF_WEEK = "Sunday" THEN WRITE "Visit friends!"
```

Remember not to include the % (percent) sign in the IF . . . THEN statements. DAY_OF_WEEK should be in ALL CAPS to work properly.

9. Set up your login script to display the listing for your home directory using the DOS DIR command. An example of this is:

```
#COMMAND/C DIR H:
```

Make sure that this command does not come before the MAP statement you have already entered for drive H:, otherwise, the system will not know to what H: is pointing.

10. You may come back to the EXIT command after you complete Chapter 11. At this time, save your login script by pressing "escape." After saving your login script, exit NETADMIN quickly by pressing Alt F10. Log out and then log in again to determine if your login script will work correctly.

11. When you log in to the network, notice any errors that occur during the execution of your login script. Return to your login script screen and correct any problems you noticed.

CHAPTER ELEVEN

MENUS

INSPIRING MOMENT

Time seems to pass so quickly at your new position. You really enjoy working with NetWare 4.1 networks, but you are exhausted. The particular company for which you are working uses quite a few temporary helpers for administrative tasks such as keying in customer names and addresses for mailings, entering inventory control data, and processing mail correspondence. Your supervisor has asked you to be in charge of the temporary workers. They are quite skilled at using the keyboard, but most of them do not know anything about networks. You are constantly having to show them where to find various software applications and how to run commonly used routine commands. There has got to be an easier way.

QUESTIONS FOR THOUGHT

Could an automated menu system help in this situation? What kinds of things would you put in an automated menu system for new users to select? What kinds of tasks do users perform on the network every day? Could an automated menu system help new users find their way around the network even if they do not know how the directories are laid out? Could an automated menu system lessen the amount of user errors that normally occur on a network? Could an automated menu system help existing users? If so, in what ways? Could you benefit from an automated menu system?

CHALLENGE

Menus save time and also lessen the stress normally associated with training users how to use the network. Explore the steps needed for creating menus and practice them as much as you can. Make a list of things you do on the LAN routinely and experiment with creating menus that will allow you to do these tasks more efficiently. Check with your LAN administrator to see if there are some already-created menus for practice. Reviewing other users' menus is also an effective way to develop the art of creating menus. Creating menus is an art, not a science, so be creative and design some menus.

OBJECTIVES

After finishing this chapter, you should be able to:

1. Explore how menus are constructed and create a menu.

2. List the rights necessary to create a menu.

3. List the rights necessary to use a menu.

4. Explain menu syntax.

NETWARE MENUS

Menus provide a powerful way to automate command and program selections. This chapter is particularly helpful in showing users how to speed up daily work, especially if particular programs or commands are used frequently. Menus are also handy when training people who do not have NetWare experience to get to needed programs or run needed commands. Unlike many programming languages today, users can construct menus in very little time with very little training. This ease of creating and using menus makes NetWare menus unique.

RIGHTS REQUIRED TO CREATE MENUS

To create a menu, a user must have trustee directory rights to the directory on which he or she wishes to place a menu. The rights required for the directory into which a user wishes to place the menu are

> Read (R)
> File scan (F)
> Write (W)
> Create (C)
> Erase (E)

In addition to the directory required for creating the menu, a user needs to have access to a directory in which the system will place temporary controlling files. This directory itself is not temporary, but the controlling files that the system creates during the running of the menu are. The user must have the following rights to the directory that will be used for the temporary controlling files:

> Read (R)
> File scan (F)
> Create (C)

Modify (M)

Erase (E)

REQUIREMENTS FOR RUNNING A MENU

The network operating system (NOS) creates and uses temporary files while running a menu. The SET command,

```
SET S_FILEDIR = F:\MENUAREA\
```

is used to specify into which directory the NOS should place these files. This command may be keyed in at any prompt, such as the F:\> prompt. The administrator of an organization's LAN should create a common directory for all users on the system. To ensure that the NOS is accessing the same directory for each user, the following SET command should be added to the container login scripts:

```
SET S_FILEDIR = "F:\MENUAREA\"
```

Notice that if the command is placed in a login script, quotation marks must be placed around the directory path. If the SET command is manually keyed in at a prompt, the quotation marks are excluded. (Menus and accompanying SET commands can be either processed manually at the prompt or automated in a login script.) The administrator should ensure that trustee directory rights RWCEMF (read, write, create, erase, modify, and filescan) were assigned.

In addition to specifying the directory name for temporary menu use, the administrator may also want to specify the temporary file name. This is done by placing the following SET command in the container login script:

```
SET S_FILE = "%STATION"
```

This command helps avoid problems encountered when two users log in at the same time with the same login name. For example, if everyone in the Accounting Department logs in the same way, such as "LOGIN ACCT," a problem with the menus would most likely occur. By default, the system would take the user's login name as the temporary file name to use. In the above SET command, "%STATION" indicates that the station connection number should be used as the temporary file name. Because no two users can log in to the same connection number on the same network, each user's temporary file would have a unique name.

ADVANTAGES TO USING MENUS

Menus provide a user a way to automate the selection process. Selections can range from running a DOS or NetWare command to running a software application.

Menus are particularly useful when working on a LAN. Because a user can have mapped drives up to the letter Z: and because many directories can be set up, menus provide a convenient way to access software easily without having to think every time about where the files are located. By providing selections in an organized manner, menus also provide a way to train new users.

```
MENU 01, Title{}
        ITEM Choice or Option{}
                commands
        ITEM Choice or Option{}
                commands
        ITEM Choice or Option{}
                SHOW 02
MENU 02, lower menu title{}
        ITEM Choice or Option{}
                commands
```

FIGURE 11.1
Order for menu construction.

SAMPLE MENU

Figure 11.1 shows the order for menu construction. The menu title goes first, and it is usually lined up on the left margin. The second line begins with the word *"item,"* and it contains a choice or selection option that is usually indented one tab stop from the left margin. Whatever is keyed on the second line becomes an option on the menu. The lines indented, usually two tab stops, that follow the choice line are made up of commands. The computer executes these commands whenever that choice is selected. Notice that lower-level menus can be called from the main menu, as shown in Figure 11.2.

Figure 11.3 shows a sample menu based on Figure 11.2. NetWare automatically puts the choices in alphabetical order. Figure 11.4 shows the sample's lower menu when the artist menu of Figure 11.3 is chosen.

Executing a Menu

To execute a menu, "NMENU" followed by the name of the menu should be keyed in. For example, to run a menu located in the user's home directory, key in as follows:

```
H:\USERS\USER01>NMENU MUSIC
```

If this particular menu should appear automatically each time the user logs in, add the following lines to the end of the user's login script:

```
MAP H:=SYS:USERS\USER01
EXIT "NOW.BAT"
```

```
MENU 01, Music Man{}
        ITEM Records and Hits{}
                EXEC MUSIC.EXE
        ITEM Sheet Music{}
                EXEC SOLOS.EXE
        ITEM Music Books{}
                EXEC BOOKS.EXE
        ITEM Artist Menu{}
                SHOW 02
MENU 02, Performers{}
        ITEM Lookup by Name{}
                EXEC NAME.EXE
        ITEM Lookup by Song{}
                EXEC SONG.EXE
```

FIGURE 11.2
Menu script file.

```
Music Man
_____
| Artist Menu
| Music Books
| Records and Hits
| Sheet Music
```

FIGURE 11.3
Sample menu when executed.

```
Performers
_____
| Lookup by Name
| Lookup by Song
```

FIGURE 11.4
The lower menu of Figure 11.3, if the artist menu is chosen.

Planning, Creating, and Implementing a Menu System

1. **Planning**

   Design on paper what the menu should look like. What should happen when each selection is chosen?

2. **Create a Common Directory to Hold Temporary Files**

   This common directory allows the network operating system access to creating temporary files while processing menus.

3. **Assign Users RWCEMF Rights to the Common Directory**

   READ, WRITE, CREATE, ERASE, MODIFY, and FILE SCAN rights to the common directory created in step 2 need to be assigned.

4. **Decide the Placement of the Menu**

   Decide where the actual menu will be created and stored. Create a directory for the menu(s) that are shared among users.

5. **Assign RFWCE Rights to the User Creating the Menu**

   READ, FILE SCAN, WRITE, CREATE, and ERASE rights need to be assigned to the user creating the menu. The rights should be assigned for the directory mentioned in step 4.

6. **The Creator of the Menu Will Now Change to the Directory**

   To make sure that the menu will get stored in the proper directory, the creator of the menu will change to the directory mentioned in step 4 (for example: F:\MENUS\ACCT>).

7. **Assign R and F Rights to the Users Executing the Menu**

   Grant users READ and FILE SCAN rights to the directory mentioned in step 4 so that users can run the menu(s).

8. **Create the Menu Script File**

   To create the menu, use an ASCII editor such as the DOS EDIT command (F:\MENUS\ACCT>EDIT TOOLS.SRC). When the edit screen comes up, key in the menu.

FIGURE 11.5
Setting up a menu system (part 1 of 2).

Use the DOS editor to create the batch file NOW.BAT. The batch file contains the command for executing the menu:

```
H:\USERS\USER01>EDIT NOW.BAT
NMENU H:MUSIC
```

See Chapter 2 for more information about the DOS editor.

9. **Compile the Menu Script File**

Use F:\MENUS\ACCT>MENUMAKE TOOLS.
Note: If the menu script file's extension is SRC, the extension does not have to be keyed in after the file name when using the MENUMAKE command line utility (CLU). The compiling process produces a file with the extension DAT.

10. **Update the User's Login Script**

Include the two SET commands in the user's login script:
SET S_FILEDIR = "F:\MENUAREA\" and SET S_FILE = "%STATION."

11. **Log In**

Log in to test the user's account.

12. **Test Run the Menu**

Use F:\>NMENU TOOLS. It is not necessary to include the DAT extension.

13. **Troubleshooting**

If the menu does not work properly, go back through the steps and debug each step that did not work correctly. *Special reminder:* If any changes are made to the ASCII file, don't forget to recompile the menu.

14. **Automate a Menu (Optional)**

The following lines may help automate a menu further by instructing the system to execute a menu automatically when the user logs in.

a. In the login script, include the lines:
MAP INS S3: = ABC_SYS:MENUS\ACCT
EXIT "GOMENU"
b. Change the directory to the location of the menu and create a small batch file.
F:\>CD \MENUS\ACCT
F:\MENUS\ACCT>EDIT GOMENU.BAT
NMENU H:TOOLS
c. Log out, then log back in to test if the menu will now appear automatically when the login script is executed.

EXEC Command

When writing menus, the EXEC command should be used to execute .EXE and .COM files from within a menu.

The steps for developing a menu system are shown in Figure 11.5. Each step is necessary to plan, create, and implement a menu system.

AUTOMATING A MENU

The following lines may help automate a menu further:

1. In the container login script, include these lines

```
MAP INS S3: = ABC_SYS:MENUS\ACCT
EXIT "GOMENU"
```

2. Change the directory to the location of the menu and create a small batch file:

```
F:\>CD \MENUS\ACCT
F:\MENUS\ACCT>COPY CON GOMENU.BAT
NMENU H:TOOLS
```

Press "CTRL Z" and "enter" to save the batch file.

3. Log out, then log in again to test if the menu will now appear automatically when the login script is executed. *Note:* You must log in to the account for which the menu was created to see the results. You must log in again because the login script changes that were made do not take effect until the next login session.

SUMMARY

Extensive programming is not required to construct NetWare menus. By following the simple guidelines presented in this chapter regarding required rights and the placement of the menu titles, choices, and commands, users can easily construct their own menus.

The following rules help when creating menus:

1. The word "menu nn" (where nn is a number) appears on the first line to indicate the menu title. Titles line up with the left margin.
2. Options/selections start with the word "item." These choices are like a description. Although options lines are normally indented, they do not have to be.
3. After each option, the commands needed for that option are listed. Commands are normally indented from the left margin two tab stops.

EXERCISES

1. Define the following:
   (a) menu
   (b) menu script file
   (c) menu title
   (d) menu item
   (e) directory containing temporary system-created files
   (f) temporary file
2. What do the following mean in NetWare?
   (a) S_FILEDIR
   (b) S_FILE
   (c) %STATION
   (d) EXEC
   (e) ITEM
3. What rights are required to create a menu?

4. What rights are required to run a menu?
5. What are the benefits of setting up menus?
6. What goes on the first line of a menu?
7. What goes on the second line of a menu?
8. What goes on the third line of a menu?
9. What type of files can be executed by the EXEC command?

LAB 11

In this lab, you will explore an already-existing menu, then you will create a menu on your own. By the end of this lab, you should feel comfortable with menus and be able to create menus and explain the instructions found in them.

1. Use the NetWare COPY command to copy the menu called MAIN.SRC to your home directory. (MAIN.SRC comes with the NetWare software.) Give it a new name.

   ```
   F:\PUBLIC>NCOPY MAIN.SRC \USERS\USERxx\TRYIT.SRC
   ```

2. Next, go to your home directory. Follow the steps for compiling and executing the menu TRYIT.SRC.
3. You should now see different selections on the menu. Try each selection, one at a time. Make notes on what each selection is doing.
4. Now create a menu of your own. Automate the selection of commonly used NetWare commands, or whatever else you deem appropriate. You may want to assign a map to software application directories that contain word processing or spreadsheets. After you assign the maps, set up a menu to run these applications.

EXPLORING SOFTWARE

This part explores common questions and terminology encountered when selecting software for a LAN. Suggestions for finding information on software applications are also discussed.

CHAPTER TWELVE

SELECTING SOFTWARE

INSPIRING MOMENT

As part of your job as a LAN administrator, you are responsible for keeping the directories and files on the file server's volumes organized and manageable. Many users share the file server's hard drive. You are now in the midst of a storage crisis. The hard drives on the file server are full, and many applications are no longer in use. Users have dumped hundreds of miscellaneous files onto the drives, ranging from games to obscene files to important business-related files. Your supervisor wants you to ensure that directory structures are organized and maintained.

QUESTIONS FOR THOUGHT

How would you decide which software to put and/or keep on your network? How would you decide which software to put and/or keep on your workstations? How would you monitor piracy on your network and workstations? What would you do if your users were bringing in their own software and putting it on the network or on their workstation? How would you educate users about your company's policy on piracy and copying software?

CHALLENGE

Keep the network clean. The network administrator should have written guidelines in place regarding what is and is not allowed on the network. An organization is a professional place for conducting business, and obscenity should not be tolerated. To determine whether or not games and other personal software should be permitted on the network or workstations, ask yourself the following question: Is your organization licensed to do so?

OBJECTIVES

After finishing this chapter, you should be able to:

1. Identify different categories of software and the major purpose of each category.
2. Know how to choose the source or vendor from which to buy software.

3. Know how to decide among software alternatives.

4. Identify where to go for further information on software.

5. Determine how many workstations can use a particular software package.

6. Know what software metering is and why it is important.

7. Identify different uses for software today.

SELECTING AND BUYING SOFTWARE

Once accounts have been set up, decisions about selecting and buying software need to be made. This chapter provides guidelines to help choose the software that's right for an organization. Because the need for sharing software among various workstations is a major reason companies choose to have a local area network, this chapter is filled with tips on getting the best software and buying it from the most reliable source.

DETERMINING HOW MANY WORKSTATIONS CAN USE SOFTWARE

Some manufacturers produce single-user software applications that will run in a LAN environment with the understanding and agreement that when such software is purchased, it will only be used by one workstation (or personal computer). The manufacturers' intention is to charge a fee for each workstation that uses the software. Technically, many single-user software programs on the market today may actually be used by more than one workstation; there may be less security and control available for the LAN and less customization for individual users than software used at only one workstation, however, because the same single-user software is being used. Some manufacturers may also add programming instructions specifically to limit the number of workstations that have access to the software. The best precaution is not to use single-user software as though it were multiuser software.

If an organization does purchase single-user software and then wants to allow more workstations access to it, the manufacturer or the software vendor should be consulted. There are four ways that manufacturers grant permission for more workstations to use such software.

First, some manufacturers require a separate software application package to be bought for each workstation, with each package costing the same price. The advantage is that each user would have his or her own manuals or documentation. The disadvantage is that this approach is generally expensive, especially if there are many individual users. Usually, only one set of software is installed with this type of purchase. By buying extra software application packages, the manufacturer is granting permission for other workstations to use the already-installed software.

The second way some manufacturers allow organizations to obtain permission to use software on more than one station is to require the purchase of a certificate or manual for each additional station. The certificate shows that the proper fees have been paid to access the software set already installed. This method is similar to the first except that the purchase of the entire software package for each station is not required.

The third method that software manufacturers use to allow permission for more than one workstation to use software is by the use of LAN packs. First, the single-user software application package is purchased; in addition, LAN packs are purchased to allow for more workstations. A LAN pack generally allows a group of users to be added. For example, a LAN pack of five would grant permission for five more workstations to use the software. This approach offers advantages to both software manufacturers and users. With LAN packs in use, there is more control of exactly how many workstations can use the software, making it more profitable for the manufacturer and offering more security for users. LAN packs also often allow users to customize their own environments; that is, if one user wants a blue screen and another wants a green one, each screen can be changed. Another benefit of LAN packs is their flexibility in allowing users to work with the same shared file. LAN packs, as of now, may be the most practical choice for an organization to use software at more than one workstation legally.

A fourth method of gaining permission is to purchase a corporate or site license agreement either directly from the manufacturer or through a value-added reseller (VAR), who represents the manufacturer. When a site license is purchased, the maximum number of users allowed to run the software is agreed upon, either in writing or through controlling within the software itself. Site license software would then be delivered to the company or organization by the VAR or the software manufacturer. Site license software packs are not commonly seen displayed on computer store shelves.

Software Metering

When selecting software for a LAN environment, the term *software metering* often emerges, especially in companies where security is highly regulated. Software metering involves counting how many users are logged in to the network and are using a particular software application. Once the count has been taken, it is then checked against licensing information to see if the number of licensed stations running the software has been exceeded. Software metering is accomplished through special software that is loaded at the file server or administrator's workstation. Various companies sell add-on software metering programs.

Why Is Software Metering Important?

Suppose that an organization just purchased a software application with a licensing agreement for 10 people to use it at a time. As these users work at their stations, an eleventh person logs in and attempts to use the software. Even if the software application program does not start flashing red alert messages, the organization now has one user running the software illegally. Software metering alerts the administrator, who could then check to see if all the users requesting to use that particular software application are actually using it. For instance, if one user simply forgot to exit the program, the administrator can ask that user to exit so that another person can use it legally.

DECIDING WHERE TO PURCHASE SOFTWARE

Numerous places sell software. Some considerations that may help in the decision of where to purchase software are the following:

1. How long has the company selling the software been in business, and will it stay in business? Although number of years in the business is not the only criteria, it is a plus if the company has been in business for a while. Avoid shopping for software at going-out-of-business sales unless you already know about the software you are purchasing, plan on keeping it, and don't intend to have any questions for the software vendor.
2. How much does the software cost at this particular location? Although price is a big factor, make sure that a low price does not entail the sacrifice of service.
3. Does the person buying the software know anyone else who buys products from this particular source? Software should be bought from a store that has a good reputation. It's a good practice to get referrals.
4. What is the software supplier's return policy? Some stores take back software with no questions asked. Some will allow a specific number of days to try the software; after that time has expired, the software cannot be returned. Some give cash back, while others give in-store credit.
5. What type of support does the store offer? To compete for business, some stores require that their employees be knowledgeable in the use of various software applications. Ask or observe if the salespeople can answer questions or can help if a software problem develops.
6. What type of purchase plans are available? In working with software purchases for a LAN environment, the cost can vary depending on the number of workstations. Many companies, especially those with more workstations, have procedures for computer purchases. It is advisable to first check with the organization about how computer purchases are processed, and then find a store that is willing to cooperate with that process. Does the organization pay direct, with cash or check? Does the company require a purchase order? Do the payments need to be stretched over time?
7. Does the store offer any special training classes? To compete for business, some stores have training available. A nominal fee may be charged.

DETERMINING SOFTWARE'S USE

Before shopping for software, an inventory of what the software should accomplish is necessary. The following categories of software should be considered.

Word-Processing Software

Word-processing software allows a user to produce many documents, from simple letters to sophisticated publishing packages. Tasks that currently require editing, correspondence, and so forth, as well as upcoming projects, should be listed. When shopping for any software, poll the people who will actually be using it about their needs.

Spreadsheet Software

Spreadsheets allow for mathematical calculations in a column format. In addition, such software allows graphs to be created to depict the numbers and calculations.

Database Management Software

Database management allows for the management of records. It allows a user to produce reports and labels based on the records. Many database management software packages have the capability of allowing a company to set up a menu system from which to choose options.

Desktop Publishing Software

Desktop publishing involves the use of graphics, special layouts, and special type fonts. Desktop publishing software is highly useful if a company produces its own advertisements, announcements, newsletters, and other written materials. Newer word-processing software applications overlap in this area in that they also have some publishing capabilities.

Accounting Software

There are numerous choices in accounting software from which to choose. As the word *accounting* implies, this category of software allows a company to manage its financial records. Although database and spreadsheet software have accounting capabilities, accounting software applications are generally already set up for financial purposes. With database or spreadsheet software, the user or company's programmer/operator must set up the financial system before it can be used.

Modem Software

Computerized dial-in bulletin boards, on-line services, and the Internet are all popular methods of communicating via a computer. Modem software enables one computer to call out to another through the use of a special device called a modem. Special software is required to operate or control a modem. Modems sold on the market today usually come packaged with sample software.

Integrated Packages

The field of integrated packages is the hot area in software development today. Integrated packages combine different categories of software such as word processing, spreadsheets, and database management from one vendor and sell it all together. Software vendors are usually involved in pricing wars to attract customers so that a user buys all the packages from the "winning" vendor. Advantages of this strategy for customers are price savings, compatibility among packages, one source to contact for support, and neat packaging.

Computer-Aided Design and Computer-Aided Mapping Software

Computer-aided design (CAD) and computer-aided mapping (CAM) software allow a user to design blueprints using a computer. These software programs are popular with architects and engineers.

Education Software

Many excellent educational software programs, from learning how to speak another language to learning how to cook, are available for use on a computer. Before shopping for this kind of software, make an inventory of the users' and company's needs to save time, confusion, and money.

DECIDING WHAT SOFTWARE TO BUY

The following steps should be helpful when looking for software and all the programs look good. The following should help narrow down your choices to just a few.

1. Check the inventory list before shopping. Which software alternatives have the capability to meet all or most of the needs or features that you originally wrote down? If the software cannot do what you need it to do, keep looking until you find one that does. Otherwise, you may become frustrated and waste time and money.
2. Check out the software manufacturer just like you checked out the store from which to buy the software. How long has the software manufacturer been in business? How long has it been producing this type of software? Does the manufacturer offer any guarantees? Are there any customer-support phone lines? If so, is it toll free or not? Does the software manufacturer charge a consulting fee to answer your questions? If so, how much? Do you know anyone who has purchased software manufactured by this company? Ask the store salesperson which software applications produce the most sales.
3. Check training and support materials. How can you learn to use this particular software? Is the software difficult to learn? Are there any classes for this software in your area? Are there any magazines or newsletters that support this particular software application? How many books are available on this particular software?
4. Check if the software will run on your computer equipment. Do you have enough random-access memory (RAM)? Do you have a large enough storage space (hard drive)? Do you have a fast enough central processing unit (CPU) (286, 386, 486, 586, . . .)? If needed, will your monitor support special graphics? Do you have the right operating system (DOS, Windows, . . .)? Is it for stand-alones, single users? Is it network compatible or NetWare aware?

FINDING FURTHER INFORMATION ON SOFTWARE

With software constantly changing, it's difficult to stay current on all the features and capabilities available. Some resources are available to help stay in the lead on these issues, however, such as publications and other users.

Magazines

There are numerous magazines written for computer users. Several such magazines test various software, report main features, and compare software applications currently available. Several software publishers refer to these tests and reviews on their software packages. In addition, many software publishers advertise in the magazines and give information about acquiring demo disks of their products.

User Groups

Scattered throughout the United States are various user groups that meet to discuss various computer issues. Some groups are general in nature and address a variety of software choices, while others are more specialized. Because user groups normally are not in the business of selling software, they often provide more straightforward answers to your questions than manufacturers and suppliers.

Bulletin Board Service

Several software manufacturers have bulletin board services (BBSs) set up where users can dial up via modem and retrieve information on their products. Some charge for this service.

The Internet

The Internet allows users around the world to exchange information via modems and satellites. The Internet has an overwhelming amount of information regarding computer hardware and software. Many software manufacturers, libraries, schools, and businesses have accounts on the Internet and have set up information centers commonly called web sites that users can access.

Computer Stores

Local computer stores are also a resource for answering questions. Find out which software applications are recommended, and which ones produce the most sales.

Libraries

Most libraries carry computer books, and many will track down books for patrons. It's wise to find software applications that have books and documentation available for users.

Software Manufacturers

Most software publishers supply literature, customer support, and/or fax help. Call a particular manufacturer to see what's available.

SUMMARY

Selecting software is not always easy. But by following a few simple guidelines, the task is quite manageable. The needs of the users and the company should be determined before shopping begins. Vendors or stores that sell the software, as well as the software manufacturer, should be checked thoroughly. Many resources, such as publications and other users, can help answer questions.

EXERCISES

1. Define the following:
   (a) single-user software
   (b) software metering
   (c) LAN pack
   (d) return policy
   (e) purchase plan
   (f) categories of software
   (g) integrated package
   (h) user groups
   (i) bulletin board service
   (j) Internet

2. What do the following mean?
   (a) RAM
   (b) CPU
   (c) VGA
   (d) SVGA
   (e) BBS

3. Why is selecting the right software important in a LAN environment?
4. What determines how many workstations can legally use the software? What are the four ways manufacturers grant permission to use their software on the LAN?
5. What are some things to keep in mind when deciding on where to buy software?
6. What categories of software are available? List the software applications with which you are familiar and the category of each.
7. How can you decide among three or four alternative software applications?
8. Where can you find more information regarding a particular kind of software?

SPECIAL PROJECT

In the following project, you will investigate the software set up on the network you are currently using. You will also explore and practice the software selection process. After completing this project, you should have a greater understanding of the software currently residing on the network. You should also be comfortable selecting software and selecting where to buy software.

1. In prior labs, you discovered which directories are entrusted to you. Now that you know your trustee directory assignments, list the directories, what type of application is contained (if any), and to what use you would put the application.
2. Which software applications mentioned in step 1 can be used by more than one user at the same time?
3. For each software application listed in step 1, can you think of another software application that could also meet the needs of the organization?
4. Write down which company actually manufactured each application listed in step 1.
5. List the names of computer stores in your area that might carry the software application that you are using and the ones mentioned as alternatives in step 3.
6. Pick one of the vendors mentioned in step 5 and answer these questions:

   How long has the company selling the software been in business, and will it stay in business?

   How much does the software cost at this particular location?

   Do you know anyone else who buys products from this particular source?

   What is this vendor's return policy?

   What type of support does the store offer?

   What type of purchase plans are available?

   Does the store offer any special training classes?

7. Pick one of the software applications listed in step 1 and find magazine articles about it.
8. Look through local trade magazines for user groups that meet to discuss any of the applications mentioned in step 1. Find as many as possible.
9. Do any of the organizations mentioned in step 8 support or encourage a particular bulletin board service or Internet address?
10. List the libraries in your area that have or can obtain computer books.

FOR FURTHER LEARNING

MAGAZINES RELATING TO NETWORKING

LAN, The Network Solutions Magazine
Miller Freeman Publications
P.O. Box 58123
Boulder, CO 80322-8124
(800) 234-9573 or (303) 447-9330
Internet home page: http://www.lanmag.com

LAN Times
1900 O'Farrell St., Suite 200
San Mateo, CA 94403
(800) 525-5003
(415) 513-6800 or fax (415) 513-6985
Internet home page: http://www.wcmh.com

NetWare Solutions
10711 Burnet Rd., Suite 305
Austin, TX 78758-4459
(512) 873-7761 or fax (512) 873-7782
Internet e-mail address: 75730.2465@compuserve.com

MAGAZINES RELATING TO PERSONAL COMPUTERS IN GENERAL

Computer Currents
5720 Hollis St.
Emeryville, CA 94608
(510) 547-6800 or fax (510) 547-4613
Internet home page: http://www.currents.net

InfoWorld
P.O. Box 1164
Skokie, IL 60076-8164
(415) 572-7341 or (800) 227-8365
Internet home page: http://www.infoworld.com

INTERESTING WEBSITES ON THE INTERNET

Digital Equipment
http://www.digital.com

IBM
http://www.ibm.com

Intel Corporation
http://www.intel/com

McAfee Associates
http://www.mcafee.com

Microsoft
http://www.microsoft.com

Novell
http://www.novell.com

Prentice Hall
http://www.prenhall.com

ERROR MESSAGES

BAD COMMAND OR FILE NAME

The "bad command or file name" error message is commonly displayed after a user has accidentally keyed in a command, such as WHOAMI, with spelling errors.

DIRECTORY COULD NOT BE LOCATED

The "directory could not be located" error message normally comes up if a user is trying to change to a directory that does not exist or if the user has not been assigned trustee directory rights to the directory.

FILE CANNOT BE COPIED ONTO ITSELF

The "file cannot be copied onto itself" message usually occurs when a user is using the NCOPY or COPY command incorrectly. The copy commands require the user to specify the source (where the file is coming from) and the destination (where the file is going). This error message normally occurs if the same directory path and file name were entered as part of the command.

INVALID DRIVE SPECIFICATION

The "invalid drive specification" message indicates that the workstation is unable to connect to a particular drive letter. If this message occurs while attempting to attach to the workstation to the network, the error is usually associated with either cabling or connection problems. To rectify the problem, check the cables and connections for the workstation encountering the error message. If an entire string of workstations is encountering this error message, check the connections leading to the hub or concentrator. Check to ensure that the power to the concentrator or hub is working properly. If all stations are encountering this message, check the terminators, if any, on the backbone, the main cable running throughout the network. If all else fails, check the file server itself.

If the "invalid drive specification" message is not a result of cabling or connection problems, perhaps the drive letter to which the user is attempting to switch or reference has not been assigned. For example, if the user is at F:\> and is trying to switch to P:\> without having a map assignment to P:, the drive P: is unknown to the system and thus is invalid.

PATH/FILE ACCESS ERROR

The "path/file access error" message is commonly encountered when attempting to save by using the DOS EDIT command. This message is conveying to the user that the system is not allowing a WRITE instruction to occur. This happens if the user either does not have enough rights assigned to the particular directory, if the particular files already exist and contain an attribute flag of read-only, or if the user's work disk is write protected.

THE COMMAND LINE SYNTAX IS INVALID

The "command line syntax is invalid" message indicates that the user has a typing mistake in the command just entered.

YOUR CURRENT CONTEXT IS ABC_CO.CONSULTANTS; THE USER DOES NOT EXIST IN THE SPECIFIED CONTEXT; ACCESS HAS BEEN DENIED

The "user does not exist" message occurs when logging in. If the system cannot find the particular account by the name that the user is entering, this error message appears on the screen. This could be the result of keying in the log in name incorrectly or of not having the context set to the right container.

YOUR CURRENT CONTEXT IS ABC_CO.CONSULTANTS; ACCESS HAS BEEN DENIED

The "access has been denied" message, when not accompanied by "the user does not exist" message, indicates that the password has been entered incorrectly when logging in.

GLOSSARY

Access Control   A right that allows a user to control who has access to a particular directory. The user can also change the IRF. If a user has access control but no supervisory privileges, and if an IRF is placed on the directory, the user cannot change the IRF back without the help of an administrator or someone with supervisory directory rights.

Attach   What happens when the workstation is identified as part of the network by the file server. Attaching occurs even before the logging in process. A user can be attached, but not actually logged in to, the network.

Backbone   The main cabling running through the entire local area network.

BBS   See *Bulletin board service.*

Bridge   A method of using special hardware and software to allow two LANs to connect together.

Bulletin Board Service (BBS)   An electronic bulletin accessed via modem. Many public and private organizations have bulletin boards into which users can dial with their modems and obtain information or assistance.

Bus Topology   The physical layout or arrangement of cabling for the LAN in which workstations are normally connected in a straight line, one after the other. The ends of the lines are capped off with what is referred to as a terminator; this marks the end of the bus.

Cabling/Cables   The wires (cables) used in physically connecting all the workstations and the file server to the network.

Cache   Fast-speed RAM that allows for faster processing of key data. Items used most often are placed here.

Carrier Sense Multiple Access/Collision Detection (CSMA/CD)   A particular access method regulating how data are sent on the network. The workstation's NIC must look to see if the channel (cable path) is busy before sending any data packets to the file server. If more than one workstation sends data packets at the same time and there is a "data collision," the network detects this, and the workstations' NICs will resend.

Centralized Processing   A method of processing applications and user requests at a central location. This type of processing is commonly found in mainframe environments.

Central Processing Unit (CPU)   The main processing unit of the computer, often referred to as the "brain." It receives commands and instructions and carries out the requests.

Client   The platform that requests data. See *Host.*

CLU   See *Command line utility.*

Command Line Utility (CLU)   Executable programs produced by Novell. For example, user CLUs are located in the PUBLIC directory. User CLUs include MAP, SEND, NDIR, and FLAG.

Concentrator   A central meeting point. Most commonly, it is an intelligent wiring center with sophisticated network management capabilities that can run multiple cable types and topologies simultaneously. A concentrator allows workstations to be tied into the backbone of the network.

Container Login Script   The script that executes first after logging in. Created by the administrator, it is normally associated with an organization or department and usually follows the hierarchical structure of the company.

Containers   Logical divisions of NDS, used for grouping and organizational purposes. Three types of containers are country, organization, and organizational unit.

CPU   See *Central processing unit.*

Create   The right required by a user to be allowed to make a new file.

CSMA/CD   See *Carrier sense multiple access/collision detection.*

Current Context   The position in the NDS tree at which a user is currently located when logged in to the network.

Decentralized Processing   A method of processing applications and user requests at a local workstation location. The actual work processing takes place at the workstation by that workstation's CPU. This type of processing is commonly found in LAN environments.

Dedicated File Server   A computer that constantly acts as a servant to the workstations by sharing resources and serving files.

Default Login Script   If a user does not have a personal login script, the default login script, which is built into the LOGIN.EXE executable file, will run in lieu of it.

Disk Duplexing   Part of SFT II. Two hard drives exist in the file server. Each drive is connected to the motherboard by the *same* controller card, and identical information is written to both drives. If one drive goes out, the other drive keeps operating. To the enduser, it is as if nothing happened. If the controller card fails, however, neither drive will function.

Disk Mirroring   Part of SFT II. Two hard drives exist in the file server. Each drive is connected to the motherboard by a *separate* controller card, and identical information is written to both drives. If one drive or its controller card goes out, the other drive and controller keep operating. To the enduser, it is as if nothing happened.

Disk Operating System (DOS)   A local operating system widely used today. It controls the operation and function at the workstation level.

Disk Subsystem   A device that allows for expansion of the storage media. When the file server's hard drives are no longer sufficient to support the needs of the network, a disk subsystem allows for adding more disk drives or other storage devices.

DOS   See *Disk operating system.*

Downsizing   An organization's attempt to save financial resources by cutting back on personnel, unneeded equipment, or plants of operation.

Dummy Terminal   Workstations that do not contain a CPU for processing applications and programs as opposed to the stations that are dependent on another unit's CPU to do the actual processing. Dummy terminals are commonly used in mainframe environments.

FAT   See *File allocation table.*

File Allocation Table (FAT)   FAT keeps a record of the addresses (locations) of files stored on disk.

File Maintenance (FILER)   FILER is a NetWare menu utility that allows for the management of files and directories.

FILER   See *File maintenance.*

File Server (FS)   The computer that contains the network operating system and controls the overall operation of the LAN.

File Server Mirroring   Part of SFT III. A method of recovering operation during a power outage or hardware problem that involves the file server. If one of two file servers that are working side by side goes down, the other keeps operating. Because both servers are doing everything identically, to the enduser it looks as if everything is running normally even if one server goes down.

FS   See *File server.*

Gateway   A method of using special hardware and software to connect dissimilar platforms, such as a LAN and a mainframe, together.

Home Directory   A data directory for private use. It is common for each user on the network to have his or her own home directory. See *Shared data directory.*

Host   The platform providing data. See *Client.*

Hot Fix   Part of SFT I. If the file server receives an instruction to write something on the disk, after it does so, it will read it to confirm that the operation was successful. If not, whatever the server was trying to write to the disk is relocated to a different area of the disk because the first area has a bad spot. The bad spot is then marked as unusable.

Hub   A central meeting point, usually a wiring box to tie workstations into the backbone of the network.

Hybrid Topology   Various other topologies are integrated together to best meet the needs of the installation site.

Inherited Rights Filter (IRF)   A way to block certain rights from trickling down to lower subdirectories.

Internetwork Packet Exchange Open Data-Link Interface (IPXODI)   The communication protocol that governs how packets of data are dispersed through the network interface cards.

IPXODI   See *Internetwork packet exchange open data-link interface.*

IRF   See *Inherited rights filter.*

LAN   See *Local area network.*

LAN Driver   A software program that controls the operation of the network interface card (NIC). This software normally comes when the NIC is purchased. The manufacturer of the NIC, rather than Novell, provides the LAN driver.

Link Support Layer (LSL)   LSL acts like a switchboard operator or mediator between IPXODI and the LAN driver.

Local Area Network (LAN)   Computers connected together allowing for the sharing of hardware and software resources, the sharing of data, and communicating together.

Local Operating System (LOS)   The local operating system, such as DOS, is responsible for controlling, operating, and carrying out instructions at the workstation level.

Login Restrictions   These particular restrictions govern the login process. Common login restrictions include account disabled, account has expiration date, and limit concurrent connections.

Login Script Commands placed in a sequential order that execute upon logging in to the network. Four types of login scripts are container, profile, user/personal, and default.

Login Time Restriction The restriction that governs the time periods that a user can log in to the network. It does not govern when the user must log out. If a user logs in during the last two minutes of his or her allowable time, he or she can remain logged in indefinitely.

LOS See *Local operating system.*

LSL See *Link support layer.*

MAN See *Metropolitan area network.*

Map A way to give directions on how to get from one directory to another. A user can set up a map drive to get to a directory more quickly.

MB See *Megabytes.*

Media Another word for cabling.

MegaBytes (MB) A measurement commonly used for accounting for disk storage. The number of MB is equal to the number of kilobytes divided by 1024. The number of kilobytes is equal to the number of bytes divided by 1024. Each character on the computer requires approximately 1 byte of storage.

Menu Utility Executable programs produced by Novell. For example, user menu utilities are located in the PUBLIC directory. Examples of user menu utilities are FILER, NETADMIN, and PCONSOLE.

Mesh Topology A particular layout or arrangement of cabling in which each computer, including the file server, is connected. The connections are point to point.

Metropolitan Area Network (MAN) MANs represent the networking or tying in of LANs from surrounding cities in a metropolitan area. MANs are common with organizations that have branch offices located near each other.

NDS See *Novell Directory Services.*

Network Address Restriction A restriction that governs on which workstation(s) a user is allowed to log in.

Network Administrator Personnel who oversees the day-to-day operation of a network. By setting up and managing user accounts, controlling security, creating comfortable work environments, making sure that printers are set up and working, maintaining preventative backups, and monitoring network performance, an administrator makes sure that users can work on the LAN easily and efficiently.

Network Drive Map See *Map.*

Network Interface Card (NIC) A card that attaches to the motherboard inside the computer; considered part of the hardware group. Externally, cabling attached to the NIC allows the computer to be physically linked to the network. The NIC controls the physical aspects of sending and receiving data on the network. All workstations and the file server must have an NIC to reside on the network.

Network Operating System (NOS) The operating system associated with the file server. It is responsible for the controlling and processing instructions at the file server level. NetWare 4.1 is an example of a NOS.

NIC See *Network interface card.*

Nondedicated File Server A computer that acts as a file server only part of the time. The rest of the time, the computer doubles as a regular workstation.

NOS See *Network operating system.*

Novell Directory Services (NDS) A system for tracking all the resources on a network; a global, distributed hierarchical database. It is organized in an upside-down tree fashion with the "roots" of the tree at the top. A container is usually found off the roots.

Open Data-Link Interface The industry standard calling for networks to be flexible enough to support a variety of workstations that may be logging in to the same network.

Password Restriction Different options that an administrator can use to control password security. These options include require password, minimum password length, force periodic password change, limit grace logins, and require unique password restrictions.

PDF See *Print device file or printer definition file.*

Personal/User Login Script See *User/personal login script.*

Polling A particular access method regulating how data are sent on the network. The file server will check with each workstation, one by one, to see if there are any requests or commands that need processing.

Print Device File or Printer Definition File (PDF) A special file that specifies configurations and instructions for a selected printer.

Print Queue A waiting line for print jobs that are waiting to print.

Print Server A computer designated for managing the printers.

Profile Login Script The script that executes after the container login script. It is usually assigned to a group of users, such as managers, clerks, or programmers. This script crosses department barriers.

Purge Deleted Files Permanently deleting one or more files so as to make them unsalvageable.

Queue A waiting line. See *Print queue.*

Queue Operator A person assigned to manage the print queues.

Queue Users People assigned to use a particular print queue.

RAM See *Random-access memory.*

Random-Access Memory (RAM) Temporary storage that goes away when the computer is turned off. This storage area is used during the processing of various commands. Maps are set up in RAM.

Read The right assigned to permit a user to see the contents of the file.

Rights The level to which a user has access to a given file or directory.

Ring Topology Workstations connected in a circular pattern with the file server also attached to the circle. The ends of the circle usually connect to the file server or some other central device.

Salvage Deleted Files An option that allows a user to bring back files that have been previously deleted as long as the files have not been purged. See *Purge deleted files.*

Search Drive Map Pointers set up in the workstation's RAM that allow for quick finding and executing of .EXE, .BAT, and .COM files. If a search drive map already points to a particular directory, executable files located in that directory may be called up at any prompt, without changing the directory containing those files.

Service Mode Indication about how forms are changed for different print queues.

SFT See *System fault tolerance.*

Shared Data Directory   A directory containing data for use by more than one user, as opposed to a home directory. See *Home directory.*

Shielded Twisted Pair (STP)   A form of cabling that offers a small amount of resistance to electrical interference. Very similar in appearance to a phone cable.

Software Metering   Counting how many users are logged in to the network and are using a particular software application. Once the count has been taken, it is then checked against licensing information to see if the number of licensed stations running the software has been exceeded.

Star Topology   Workstations connected in a star pattern with the file server also attached. The file server sits in the center, and each workstation connects to a hub or concentrator connected to the file server.

STP   See *Shielded twisted pair.*

System Fault Tolerance (SFT)   Different techniques and features that help keep a LAN up and running in the event of hardware problems. See *Disk duplexing, Disk mirroring, Hot fix, and File server mirroring.*

System Files   The files required to boot up a system initially. Commonly found files for workstation boot up include IO.SYS, MSDOS.SYS, and COMMAND.COM.

Terminal Emulation   A special computer card and software that allow a personal computer to emulate or act like a dummy terminal for purposes of communicating to the host computer in a centralized processing platform.

Token Passing   A particular access method regulating how data are sent on the network. A logical token (box) is passed throughout the LAN from workstation to workstation. As long as the token is empty, the workstation's NIC can put a command or request in it. If it's already full, the NIC must wait for the next token pass.

Topology   How cables are arranged or the cable layout.

Trustee   The person or account holder entrusted to use a particular directory or file.

Uninterruptible Power Supply (UPS)   A battery backup hardware device (often software driven) that allows the computer to continue running in case of a power outage or electrical spikes. UPSs vary greatly in price and features. They are commonly attached to the file server, but some companies even have them on workstations.

Unshielded Twisted Pair (UTP)   A form of cabling that offers a small amount of resistance to electrical interference. It is very similar in appearance to that of a phone cable.

UPS   See *Uninterruptible power supply.*

User/Personal Login Script   The script that executes after the profile login script (if there is one) when logging in. It is customized for the particular user logging in.

UTP   See *Unshielded twisted pair.*

Variable Replacement   A system option used in login script commands that accommodates data items (variables) that are unknown or vary when the user(s) log in. Sometimes the options for commands used in a login script may need to be changed depending on who logs in, on what computer, and when. Variable replacements accomplish this by allowing flexibility in the construction of the command. Variable replacements are preceded by a percent sign (%).

Virtual Loadable Module (VLM)   An executable file that allows a workstation to attach to the file server (network); it also allows a workstation to request different types of services.

Volume   The divisions of the file server's hard drive (or disk subsystem). It contains

NetWare software directories such as PUBLIC, SYSTEM, MAIL, LOGIN, and ETC. The volume may also contain software applications and data that users may be sharing.

Volume Space Restriction   An option that allows the amount of disk space that a user can have on the file server's hard drive or disk subsystem to be limited.

WAN   See *Wide area network.*

Wide Area Network (WAN)   A network that allows for LANs from a wider distance to connect together through the phone or satellite media. WANs are commonly used among organizations that have branch offices in different states.

Workstation (WS)   The computer at which a user sits to complete work. In a distributed processing environment, such as a LAN, the workstation's CPU usually does the actual processing of applications.

Write   The right assigned to permit a user to change the content of a file.

WS   See *Workstation.*

INDEX